ESL WORKBOOK
TO
ACCOMPANY
ANSON AND SCHWEGLER'S
The
LONGMAN HANDBOOK
for
WRITERS AND READERS

ESL WORKBOOK TO ACCOMPANY ANSON AND SCHWEGLER'S *The* LONGMAN HANDBOOK *for* WRITERS AND READERS

Ellen Bitterman

SUNY, New Paltz

An imprint of Addison Wesley Longman, Inc.

New York • Reading, Massachusetts • Menlo Park, California • Harlow, England
Don Mills, Ontario • Sydney • Mexico City • Madrid • Amsterdam

This book is dedicated to my mother, who taught me my mother tongue.

Senior Acquisitions Editor: Lisa Moore
Developmental Editor: Marcia Muth
Project Editor: Bob Ginsberg
Design Manager: Wendy Ann Fredericks
Cover Illustration: Tina Vey
Electronic Production Manager: Valerie A. Sawyer
Manufacturing Manager: Helene G. Landers
Electronic Page Makeup: Joanne Del Ben
Printer and Binder: RR Donnelley & Sons Company
Cover Printer: The Lehigh Press, Inc.

ISBN 0-673-98552-0

12345678910—DOC—99989796

Contents

To the Teacher

This workbook addresses the specific needs of ESL students, both in first-year composition programs for native English speakers and in advanced ESL writing classes. The need for specialized materials for ESL composition students is becoming increasingly evident to college composition teachers nationwide. Over the last two decades, the field of ESL in higher education has grown as more nonnative English speakers have entered colleges across the nation. Writing professionals have realized that these college students have markedly different needs from those of their native-speaking counterparts.

As educators, of course, our goal is to serve this population of students as directly and sensitively as possible. As the author of this book, my goal is to provide grammatical, syntactical, and mechanical explanations as well as practice exercises and writing topics that are instructional and challenging to the students. My hope is to provide meaningful integration of grammar into writing and ultimately to facilitate the students' writing success in their academic and professional work.

As an ancillary to *The Longman Handbook for Writers and Readers,* this workbook closely follows the concepts and format of its parent text. The explanations and examples of grammar, syntax, and mechanics, taken in sequence from the handbook chapters, are expanded upon through writing practice exercises.

Each chapter includes the following parts.

- Explanation of grammar, syntax, or mechanics with examples
- Exercise progression from isolated practice to integration in writing through three types of exercises

 Solitary exercises ask students to work independently on thematic exercises focusing on the ideas of the chapter.

 Collaborative exercises direct students to work with others on thematic exercises focusing on the ideas of the chapter.

 Paper-in-progress exercises direct students to choose from suggested topics and develop a piece of writing or to revise a paper already in progress in order to apply the particular grammatical or composition focus of the chapter.

Another feature of the workbook is the many writing selections from ESL students themselves. These writings demonstrate the correct or incorrect usage of the material in the chapter. They also are examples of the most common ESL challenges in writing. Finally, an answer key is provided in the back of the book, so the students can guide their own writing practice.

Acknowledgments

I want to express my deep appreciation to the many people who were my mental and spiritual guides throughout the writing of this workbook.

In particular, I want to acknowledge and thank Chris M. Anson and Robert A. Schwegler for their expertise in writing explanations and examples in Chapters 25, 26, 27, and 29, supplied from *The Longman Handbook for Writers and Readers*. Their clarity of text will be a helpful resource to our ESL students.

Further, I want to thank Marcia Muth, the developmental editor, for her gentle and knowing hand in advising me throughout the drafting of this workbook.

In addition, I extend my appreciation to the reviewers, Sandra Arfa, University of Wisconsin; Karissa Ashley, Scottsdale Community College; and Mary S. Benedetti, University of Cincinnati, whose invaluable insights contributed greatly to the writing of this workbook.

I want to thank my colleagues at SUNY New Paltz with whom I have developed professionally and collaborated for many years, as well as the ESL students, themselves, whose contributions are ongoing.

Finally, let me thank my husband, Richard, for watching over me, and my son, Brandon, for keeping me young.

ELLEN BITTERMAN

To the Student

The purpose of this workbook is to provide you, an ESL student of composition, a writing practice book that can help you in your continued study of English grammar and composition. This workbook is an ancillary to *The Longman Handbook for Writers and Readers,* and it closely follows its text and format. As you work in the book, you will also find it helpful to use the handbook chapters as a guide to the writing suggestions in this workbook. The chapters focus on aspects of grammar, syntax, and mechanics that are representative of the most common difficulties for a writing student like yourself.

There are three types of exercises in the book:

 Solitary exercises ask you to work independently.

 Collaborative exercises direct you to work with partners.

 Paper-in-progress exercises ask you to practice writing about topics that interest you or to revise or edit a draft you have already written.

In addition, throughout the book you will find student writing samples which, it is hoped, will both instruct and inspire you. Finally, you can use the answer key at the back of the book to guide your own writing practice. Over my years of teaching ESL, I have worked with many students like you, and I feel that I am writing to a very familiar audience. I hope that you will benefit from this workbook and enjoy your own writing process.

ESL WORKBOOK
TO
ACCOMPANY
ANSON AND SCHWEGLER'S
The
LONGMAN HANDBOOK
for
WRITERS AND READERS

USING WORDS

Articles

In using the **indefinite articles** *a* and *an*, or the **definite article** *the*, you can follow some rules and guidelines, but you need to pay attention to the many exceptions to these rules. Make sure you notice articles as you read. This will also help you to achieve a greater facility with articles. Most important, remember that the basic meaning of your sentence will still be communicated even if you choose the wrong article or if you forget to use one.

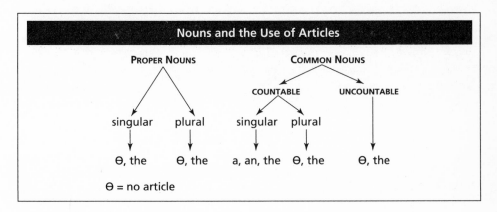

Nouns and the Use of Articles

PROPER NOUNS

COMMON NOUNS

COUNTABLE   UNCOUNTABLE

singular   plural   singular   plural

Ө, the   Ө, the   a, an, the   Ө, the   Ө, the

Ө = no article

Singular and plural proper nouns

Proper nouns use either no article or *the*. Proper nouns are capitalized and include names of people, places, religions, languages, courses of study, mountains, and rivers. (See 37b-1.)

Singular proper nouns generally use no article, and plural proper nouns usually use *the*.

NOT APPROPRIATE (SINGULAR) The Sir Francis Drake was a famous English sea captain.

CORRECT (SINGULAR) **Sir Francis Drake** was a famous English sea captain.

NOT APPROPRIATE (PLURAL) Everglades have abundant wildlife and tropical plants.

CORRECT (PLURAL) **The Everglades** have abundant wildlife and tropical plants.

Writer's Alert

Note some exceptions that require *the*.
Use *the* with national boundaries such as empires and republics.

the Roman Empire, the French Republic

Use *the* with geographical features such as rivers, oceans, and channels.

the Pacific Ocean, the English Channel

Use *the* with architectural sites such as buildings, museums, and towers.

the Coliseum, the Eiffel Tower

Exercise 1

A. Read the following sentences, which include many proper nouns. Fill in each blank before a proper noun with either *the* or *X* to show that no article is needed.

EXAMPLE   Many groups of people were early settlers in the countries of ___X___ Europe.

1. _____ England was named for _____ Angles, who merged with other invaders to become a group called _____ Anglo-Saxons.

2. _____ France was named for _____ Franks, who originally invaded that country.

3. _____ Hapsburgs ruled _____ Austria for more than six hundred years.

4. _____ Most people in _____ Italy are descended from _____ Romans.

5. _____ Minoans and _____ Mycenaeans were the first people in _____ Greece.

B. Write five to ten sentences about your country. Use as many proper nouns as you can by including information about important geographical features, leaders, cities, museums, and buildings. Exchange your sentences with a partner. Edit each other's sentences for correct article usage with proper nouns. Then go over your corrected papers together, determining the correct article usage at any points where you differ.

_____

_____

_____

_____

_____

_____

_____

_____

_____

_____

_____

_____

_____

1
art

Singular count nouns

Singular **count nouns** use *a, an,* or *the.* Remember, these nouns cannot stand alone.

NOT APPROPRIATE Pig is a very intelligent animal.

CORRECT **A pig** is a very intelligent animal.

CORRECT **The pig** is a very intelligent animal.

Plural count nouns

Plural count nouns use either no article or *the.* You should use no article to show a generalization.

NOT APPROPRIATE The books are the best teachers.

CORRECT **Books** are the best teachers.

You should use *the* with plural count nouns to refer to something specific.

NOT APPROPRIATE Books on his desk are from the library.

CORRECT **The books** on his desk are from the library.
The prepositional phrase makes the noun specific.

Exercise 2

A. Read the following sentences, which use both singular and plural countable nouns. Fill in each blank with *a, an, the,* or *X* (for no article) so that all the articles are used correctly with the nouns.

EXAMPLE ____*The*____ wolf has ____*a*____ persecuted history.

1. _____ wolf has been _____ very misunderstood animal.

2. In _____ many fairy tales, _____ wolf has been depicted as _____ ferocious animal.

3. Many people throughout history have believed that _____ wolves are _____ vicious, aggressive predators.

4. These are _____ myths about wolves.

5. _____ facts are that there are two kinds of _____ wolves: _____ red wolf and _____ gray wolf.

6. _____ basic social unit of _____ wolf population is _____ pack, and the pack lives in _____ den, which is _____ protected habitat.

7. _____ size of _____ wolf varies according to _____ geographical location.

8. In _____ spring _____ wolves have _____ pups.

9. In _____ recent years, _____ scientists have discovered _____ important role of _____ wolf in nature.

10. In fact, today we know that _____ wolves are in need of protection and that they are _____ important part of _____ ecosystem.

B. Choose one of the topics below that you know something about, and write five to ten sentences. Exchange your sentences with a partner. Edit your partner's paper for correct article usage with singular and plural nouns.

A favorite pet   A favorite relative   A favorite hobby   A favorite sport

_____

_____

_____

_____

_____

_____

_____

_____

_____

_____

_____

_____

_____

_____

_____

_____

_____

_____

_____

_____

Noncount (mass) nouns

Noncount (mass) nouns use either no article or *the*. They are never preceded by the singular article *a* or *an*.

General mass nouns sometimes stand alone.

NOT APPROPRIATE A laughter is good medicine.

CORRECT   **Laughter** is good medicine.

With specific mass nouns, use *the*.

NOT APPROPRIATE Laughter of children is good medicine.

CORRECT   **The laughter** of children is good medicine.
              The prepositional phrase makes the noun specific.

Exercise 3

A. Read the following sentences, which use uncountable nouns. Fill in each blank using *the* or *X* for no article.

EXAMPLE   Norman Cousins, an American writer, believed ___X___ laughter was ___X___ good medicine.

1. His books give _____ advice about _____ importance of having a positive mental attitude in order to recover from illnesses.

2. He believed that a state of _____ happiness and _____ well-being could help _____ healing process.

3. He maintained that _____ laughter could make a sick person well, and this gave _____ hope to many people.

4. In his own life, he had _____ courage of his convictions to write many books on this controversial subject of _____ health.

5. Norman Cousins will be remembered for having _____ strength of his beliefs to teach _____ people about a new concept of _____ healing.

B. Choose one of the following topics, and develop a short paragraph. Exchange papers with another student, and edit each other's work for correct article usage with noncount nouns.

The music of Mozart (or any other composer) or music in general
The art of the Renaissance (or any other period) or art in general
The scenery of the California coast (or any coast) or scenery in general
The advice of parents (or teachers or friends) or advice in general

_____

_____

_____

_____

_____

_____

_____

_____

1
art

_____

_____

_____

_____

_____

_____

_____

_____

_____

Strategies for choosing *a, an,* or *the*

- How do you know if you need to use *a* or *an*? When you are talking about a nonspecific, singular count noun, you use the indefinite article *a* or *an*. This means you are not referring to any specific person or thing. *A* is used before a consonant sound. *An* is used before a vowel sound.

I need to have **a car** to go to work.
The car is unknown or nonspecific. It is any car.

- How do you know if you need to use *the*? When you are talking about a specific, singular noun, you use the definite article *the*. This means you know the exact person or thing to which you are referring.

I need to have **the car** to go to work.
The car is a specific, known car.

Mr. Frank was sitting on **a beach. The beach** had sand that was unusually white.
The beach is first unknown, so the writer uses the indefinite article *a*. Then the beach is known because it has already been mentioned, so the writer uses the definite article *the*.

- Should you use *the* with plural nouns? Plural and mass nouns do not usually require any article.

COUNT   **Airline tickets** to Florida are at half price.

MASS   **Information** about flights to Florida is available.

- Should you use *the* when a plural noun is followed by a modifier? All plural count nouns and mass nouns are specific when they are followed by modifiers, and you need to use *the*.

COUNT   **The** airline tickets <u>that you bought</u> are at half price.

MASS   **The** information <u>that you received</u> about flights to Florida has changed.

In each of these sentences, the adjective clause makes the noun specific.

8

Exercise 4

A. Read the following paragraphs, and underline all the nouns. Decide whether the nouns are proper nouns, singular or plural countable nouns, or uncountable nouns, and list them in the columns below. Then edit the paragraphs by using either *a, an, the* or no article before each noun. The first sentence is done for you.

Culture Shock

Social scientists use *the* term culture shock for feelings of depression and homesickness that foreign students sometimes feel when they first live in new country. Culture shock occurs because student must adjust to new language, unfamiliar foods, different behaviors, and unusual surroundings. There are three stages that accompany experience of adjustment. During first stage, student may experience disbelief and shock. In second stage, student may feel despair and homesickness. Finally, in third stage, newcomer has more hopeful and positive attitude. He or she begins to have greater sense of identification with new country. Once culture shock is recognized, symptoms of confusion and disorientation are diffused. It is also helpful to remind students that many others are feeling similar discomfort.

Make your list of nouns here.

Proper Nouns	Singular, Countable	Plural, Countable	Uncountable
		Scientists	

_____

_____

_____

_____

_____

_____

_____

_____

_____

_____

_____

Korean Fable

Once upon time in countryside of Korea, there were father and daughter. They were living in poverty, and father couldn't make salary because he was blind. Only daughter could get small amount of money. During this time, weather was very dry, and it had not rained for long time. Therefore, people of town were looking for young woman to sacrifice her life to Dragon God in order to get rain. Daughter decided to volunteer because if she did, there would be money for her father. One day she jumped into sea from ship. From that time it rained for many days, and people could start farming. Her father could live in much richer circumstances than before, but he was very sad because his daughter had died. In sea, Dragon God was very impressed with daughter's filial duty for her father. He decided to send her back to earthly life with treasures. When father saw his daughter again, he was filled with joy. Her name was Simchung, and today, when there is person with great filial duty for parents, Korean people call person Simchung.

—Seokwan Kim, College Student

Make your list of nouns here.

Proper Nouns	Singular, Countable	Plural, Countable	Uncountable
_____	_____	_____	_____
_____	_____	_____	_____
_____	_____	_____	_____
_____	_____	_____	_____
_____	_____	_____	_____

_____

_____

_____

_____

_____

_____

_____

_____

B. Working with a partner or in a small group, compare your list of nouns with one of the paragraphs in Exercise 4a. Discuss your choice of articles.

C. For further practice with articles, go to the library and read about a city you would love to visit, an endangered species, or a famous artist, or read the following selection about the controversy over reintroducing an endangered species, the wolf, into the environment of Yellowstone National Park.

As you are reading, pay careful attention to article usage. You may even want to list the kinds of nouns you see. Then, freewrite a paragraph about your subject. Finally, edit your freewriting to correct the articles you use with all kinds of nouns.

> On the surface, the debate revolves around a simple question: How far should we go to protect and promote an endangered species that also comes into conflict with people? Yet nothing about this particular endangered species is quite that simple.
>
> The basic problem is that for people, the wolf is not just a gray doglike creature of flesh, fur and blood that roams in packs and fills the night with the music of its howls. Instead, the animal is larger than life, looming more vividly in the wilderness of the imagination than in any real forest. Sometimes, it is even a treacherous mirror, reflecting our own hidden motives and desires.
>
> —An excerpt from "Who's Afraid of the Big Bad Wolf?" by John Cary, as appeared in *National Wildlife,* August–September 1987. Copyright 1987 by the National Wildlife Federation. Reprinted with permission from National Wildlife magazines August–September issue.

As you freewrite, you may want to think about these questions.

Should we protect species that come into conflict with people?
What are our responsibilities to endangered species?
What ideas come to mind when you think about the wolf?

CHAPTER

Adjectives

Adjectives in English never use a plural form.

NOT APPROPRIATE Santo Domingo is renowned for beautiful*s* beaches.

CORRECT Santo Domingo is renowned for beautiful beaches.

Exercise 1

A. Use adjectives to add details to the following sentences.

interesting   adventurous

EXAMPLE   Scuba diving is one of the△ sports that many△ people enjoy all over the world.

1. Deep-sea diving is an adventure for people of all ages.

2. The invention of scuba gear made diving possible for people.

3. Some people become commercial divers.

4. Other divers dive for the pleasure of observing wildlife.

5. Divers can study water life and explore ships.

B. Read the following descriptive paragraph. Underline all the adjectives, and correct any errors in the form of adjectives.

A Night Dream

As I walk along the whites beaches of my lovely land, I am swept away by the beautiful scenery. The moodys waters of the sea come to the shore, always changing the perfects patterns. The maternals breezes hold me in quiet arms, and I am home again. I don't recognize any people on the beach, but their strongs faces are somehow known to me. The precious sounds of my language are heard as a soothing Spanish song. I am walking in a familiar mist. Suddenly the wind picks up, and the solitude is broken. What are these louds noises I hear? Can the oceans winds make such sounds? Am I hearing a siren on the beach?

My alarm has sounded, and another day in the busiest city in the world begins. New York, you woke me up.

—Felipe Rodriguez, College Student

2
adj

C. Together with a partner, think about city life, and add as many different adjectives as possible to the nouns in the following list.

EXAMPLE _____*musical*_____ theaters

1. _____ people   6. _____ sidewalks

2. _____ streets   7. _____ subways

3. _____ taxis   8. _____ stores

4. _____ skyscrapers   9. _____ museums

5. _____ parks   10. _____ apartments

D. Either use the list in Exercise 1c to develop a paragraph about city life, or create a new list of adjectives and nouns about country life and develop a paragraph on that topic. Try to make your writing as descriptive as possible by using adjectives. Exchange paragraphs with a partner, and circle all the adjectives you see in your partner's paragraph. Make sure the adjectives are used correctly.

2
adj

_____

_____

_____

_____

_____

_____

_____

_____

_____

_____

Prepositions

Common Prepositions					
about	as	by	in	outside	up
above	at	concerning	into	over	upon
across	before	despite	like	past	with
after	behind	down	near	through	within
against	below	during	of	to	without
along	beneath	except	off	toward	
among	between	for	on	under	
around	beyond	from	out	until	

Using prepositions in English may be difficult for you, and sometimes you will need to memorize which preposition to use. However, these guidelines can help you remember which preposition to choose.

Prepositions of time, place, and location

Prepositions of Time: *At*, *On*, and *In*.

Use *at* for a specific time.

Brandon was born **at** 11:11 a.m.

Use *on* for days and dates.

He was born **on** Monday.
My new job began **on** August eighteenth.

Use *in* for nonspecific times during a day, a month, a season, or a year.

He was born **in** the morning.
My new job began **in** August.
The weather becomes cooler **in** autumn.
The book was first published **in** 1980.

Prepositions of Place: *At, On,* and *In*.

Use *at* for specific addresses.

He works **at** 99 Tinker Street.

Use *on* for the names of streets, avenues, and boulevards.

The White House is **on** Pennsylvania Avenue.

Use *in* for the names of areas of land—counties, states, countries, and continents.

He works **in** Washington, D.C.

Prepositions of Location: *In, At, On,* and No Preposition			
IN	**AT**	**ON**	**NO PREPOSITION**
(the) bed*	class*	the bed*	downstairs
the bedroom	home	the ceiling	downtown
the car	the library*	the floor	inside
(the) class*	the office	the horse	outside
the library*	school*	the plane	upstairs
school*	work	the train	uptown

*You may sometimes use different prepositions for these locations.

Order of prepositional phrases

Use prepositional phrases in this order.

PREPOSITIONAL PHRASE OF PLACE + PREPOSITIONAL PHRASE OF TIME

         place   time
The runners will be starting **in the park on Saturday.**

Writer's Alert

When you express the idea of going to a place, use the preposition *to.*

NOT APPROPRIATE I am going work.

CORRECT I am going **to** work.

NOT APPROPRIATE I am going the office.

CORRECT I am going **to** the office.

In the following cases, use no preposition.

NOT APPROPRIATE I am going **to** home.

CORRECT I am going home.

CORRECT I am going downstairs (downtown, inside).

Exercise 1

A. Using the correct prepositions, combine the words in the following lists to write a sentence in the correct order. Make all the necessary grammatical changes.

EXAMPLE   born / Mao Tse-tung / Hunan province / December 26, 1893

Mao Tse-tung was born in Hunan Province on December 26, 1893.

1. 1963 / John F. Kennedy / assassinate / November 22 / Dallas _____

_____

_____

2. a British passenger ship / April 14 / the Titanic / 1912 / hit an iceberg _____

_____

_____

3. first walk / space / a Soviet cosmonaut / 1965 / March 18 Alexei Leonov _____

_____

_____

4. first incandescent lamp / demonstrate / October 21 / 1879 / Thomas Edison / New

York City _____

_____

_____

5. Japan / the emperor / Hirohito / became / 1926 _____

_____

_____

B. What were your first days in the United States like? Develop a paragraph about this topic. Give as much information as possible. You may develop your ideas by addressing yourself to the following questions.

How did you get to the United States?
When and where did you first arrive in the United States?
With whom did you first stay when you arrived?
Where did you stay?
When and where did you eat your first meal in the United States?
Who were the first friends you met?
Where did you meet them?

_____

_____

_____

_____

_____

_____

_____

_____

_____

_____

_____

_____

_____

_____

_____

_____

_____

For and *since* in time expressions

Use *for* with an amount of time (minutes, hours, days, months, and years).

I have lived in upstate New York **for** many years.

Use *since* with a specific date or time.

I have lived in upstate New York **since** 1974.

Exercise 2

A. Choose *for* or *since* in the following list.

1. _____ two years   6. _____ three minutes

2. _____ 1984   7. _____ yesterday

3. _____ many hours   8. _____ my birthday

4. _____ New Year's Eve   9. _____ one month

5. _____ the Civil War   10. _____ May 1, 1945

B. Write two complete sentences answering each of the following sentences, one using *for* and one using *since*. Either write your own answers, or interview another student in your class and write down those answers.

EXAMPLE   How long have you owned your car?

a. *I have owned a car for one semester.* _____

b. *I have owned a car since September.* _____

1. How long have you studied English?

a. _____

_____

b. _____

_____

2. How long have you lived in the United States?

a. _____

_____

b. _____

_____

3. How long has it been since you have spoken to your parents?

a. _____

_____

b. _____

_____

3
prep

4. How long have you been in college?

a. _____

_____

b. _____

_____

5. How long have you been living on your own?

a. _____

_____

b. _____

_____

6. How long do you plan to stay in the United States?

3
prep

a. _____

_____

b. _____

_____

C. Think of three to five questions similar to those in Exercise 2b, and interview a partner. Using the information you receive, develop a short paragraph about your partner.

_____

_____

_____

_____

_____

_____

_____

_____

_____

_____

_____

_____

Prepositions with nouns, verbs, and adjectives

Some noun-plus-preposition combinations are often found together.

noun + preposition

He has a strong **appreciation of** music.

Noun + Preposition Combinations		
approval of	fondness for	need for
awareness of	grasp of	participation in
belief in	hatred of	reason for
concern for	hope for	respect for
confusion about	interest in	success in
desire for	love of	understanding of

Some verb-plus-preposition combinations are also common.

verb + preposition

Parents **worry about** many things.

Verb + Preposition Combinations		
apologize for	give up	prepare for
ask about	grow up	study for
ask for	look for	talk about
belong to	look forward to	think about
bring up	look up	trust in
care for	make up	work for
find out	pay for	worry about

Likewise, some adjective-plus-preposition combinations are often used together.

adjective + preposition

Life in your country is **similar to** life in mine.

Adjective + Preposition Combinations		
afraid of	fond of	proud of
angry at	happy about	similar to
aware of	interested in	sorry for
capable of	jealous of	sure of
careless about	made of	tired of
familiar with	married to	worried about

Exercise 3

A. Circle the *noun* / **verb** / *adjective* + preposition combinations in the following paragraph.

Music Is a Universal Language

n.

People all over the world have a strong (appreciation of) music. A love of music has been the reason for many musical performances in many different countries. The need for music in our lives is very important no matter which country we are in. Throughout the year people look forward to classical recitals, jazz festivals, and rock concerts. It is definitely true that people of all ages have a fondness for music because music is age-less and timeless. It is also often true that people in every generation enjoy the music they are familiar with, but sometimes they are interested in new forms of music. Furthermore, people in different countries are proud of the rich musical heritage that is particular to their origins. Nonetheless, people can have a respect for and an under-standing of the music of all different countries. Indeed, music is the universal language.

3
prep

B. In the spaces below, write the combinations you found in the paragraph.

Noun + Preposition

appreciation of _____ _____ _____

_____ _____ _____ _____

_____ _____ _____ _____

Verb + Preposition

_____ _____ _____ _____

_____ _____ _____ _____

_____ _____ _____ _____

Adjective + Preposition

_____ _____ _____ _____

_____ _____ _____ _____

_____ _____ _____ _____

C. From the charts, choose five noun-, verb-, and adjective-plus-preposition combinations, and use them to write sentences.

Noun + Preposition

1. _____

_____

2. _____

_____

3. _____

_____

4. _____

_____

5. _____

_____

Verb + Preposition

6. _____

_____

7. _____

_____

8. _____

_____

9. _____

_____

10. _____

_____

Adjective + Preposition

11. _____

_____

12. _____

_____

13. _____

_____

14. _____

_____

15. _____

_____

D. Choose one of the sentences from Exercise 3c as the opening sentence for a freewriting.

_____

_____

_____

_____

_____

_____

_____

_____

_____

_____

_____

_____

_____

_____

Summary Exercise

Read the following paragraph, and choose a preposition for each space. (In some cases you may need no preposition.)

I Often Think _____ My Native Country

While I was living _____ El Salvador, I had wonderful experiences. I often went _____ my favorite places; I am reminded _____ these places _____ my daily life _____ the United States. Sometimes when I am resting _____ my room, I daydream _____ the days when I went _____ dances _____ my friends. When I go _____ the beaches here, I reminisce _____ the warm and wonderful sea _____ El Salvador. I really enjoy remembering all the adventures that I have had _____ my country. Perhaps I can go _____ there soon, and then I will bring back _____ me more memorable experiences and souvenirs.

—Edwin Hernández, College Student

USING PHRASES AND SUBORDINATE CLAUSES

CHAPTER 4

Gerunds and Infinitives

Gerunds and infinitives are verbals.

Gerund
verb (base form) + *-ing*

Infinitive
to + verb (base form)

Verbs followed by either gerunds or infinitives

You can follow some verbs with either a gerund or an infinitive, though the meaning of some of these verbs may change slightly.

GERUND
subject + verb + gerund
People   like   **socializing**   with friends.

INFINITIVE
subject + verb + infinitive
People   like   **to socialize**   with friends.

Common Verbs Taking Either Gerunds or Infinitives		
begin	intend	regret
can't stand	learn	remember
continue	like	start
forget	love	stop
hate	prefer	try

Exercise 1

A. Look at the chart titled "Common Verbs Taking Either Gerunds or Infinitives," and write sentences using some of the verbs in the list. The topic is started with the first sentence.

1. (begin) *When I first arrived in the United States, I began to immerse myself in the language and culture.*

_____

2. (can't stand) _____

_____

_____

3. (continue) _____

_____

_____

4. (forget) _____

_____

_____

5. (intend) _____

_____

_____

6. (like, love) _____

_____

_____

7. (prefer) _____

_____

_____

8. (regret) _____

_____

_____

4
ger/inf

9. (*remember*) _____

_____

_____

10. (*try*) _____

_____

_____

B. Complete the verb forms in the following sentences by adding either a gerund or an infinitive.

EXAMPLE   Human beings learn (*socialize*) ___*to socialize*___ from a very early age.

1. The process of socialization means that a new generation begins (*acquire*) _____ the knowledge, behavior, and beliefs of the older generation.

2. From an early age, adults begin (*teach*) _____ children the expected behaviors of society.

3. Children start (*recognize*) _____ and (*follow*) _____ the informal and formal rules of society.

4. They continue (*learn*) _____ the ways of society from family, peers, and school.

5. Through the process of socialization, people continue (*adapt*) _____ to the needs of society.

C. Develop a paragraph about some manners, rules, and/or behaviors that are important in your family, your school, or your country. Notice your use of gerunds and infinitives. Then exchange paragraphs with a partner, and check for gerund and infinitive usage.

_____

_____

_____

_____

_____

_____

_____

_____

_____

_____

_____

_____

_____

_____

_____

Verbs followed by gerunds

You can use only a gerund to follow some verbs.

subject + verb + gerund

GERUND   Children enjoy **reading** fairy tales.

Common Verbs Taking Gerunds		
admit	deny	mind
anticipate	discuss	miss
appreciate	dismiss	postpone
avoid	enjoy	practice
can't help	finish	quit
consider	imagine	recommend
delay	keep	suggest

Exercise 2

Look at the chart titled "Common Verbs Taking Gerunds," and write sentences using the following verbs from the list. The topic is started with the first sentence.

1. (enjoy) *People of all ages enjoy watching or participating in sports.* _____

    _____

    _____

2. (appreciate) _____

    _____

    _____

3. (can't help) _____

    _____

    _____

4. (consider) _____

    _____

    _____

5. (imagine) _____

    _____

    _____

6. (keep) _____

    _____

    _____

7. (mind) _____

    _____

    _____

8. (practice) _____

    _____

    _____

4
ger/inf

9. (*quit*) _____

_____

_____

_____

10. (*recommend*) _____

_____

_____

Idiomatic expressions using gerunds

You must use gerunds with some idiomatic expressions.

- After the word *go* (in any tense)

  subject + *go* + gerund
  I **go** shopping on Saturday.
  I **went** swimming.

- After the expression *spend time*

  subject + *spend time* + gerund
  Students **spend** a lot of **time** writing papers.
  Teachers **spend** a lot of **time** reading papers.

- After the expression *have* + noun

  subject + *have* + object + gerund
  Pilots **have** difficulty flying in bad weather.
  Shopkeepers **have** fun decorating their stores.
  Music lovers **have** a great time going to concerts.

- After a preposition

  preposition + gerund
  Veterinarians are interested **in** helping animals.
  Farmers sometimes worry **about** having an early frost.

Writer's Alert

In the following examples, the phrase beginning with *to* is not an infinitive. *To* acts like a preposition in each sentence and must be followed by a gerund ending in -*ing*.

I am looking **forward** to living abroad.
He is **accustomed** to spending time alone.
Adults are **used** to taking care of children.

Name: _____ Date: _____

Exercise 3

A. Choose one of the gerunds from the following list to complete the sentences below.

going   shopping   playing   eating   listening
swimming   walking   tending   talking   skiing

EXAMPLE   The students had fun _____*talking*_____ about their vacation plans.

1. During Christmastime many people **go** _____.

2. When it gets very hot, we always **go** _____.

3. Because we got a lot of snow last winter, we often **went** _____.

4. It is important for parents to **spend time** _____ to their children.

5. In order to get enough exercise, people should **spend time** every day _____.

6. If you want to have homegrown vegetables, you must **spend a lot of time** _____ the garden.

7. Siblings often **have a good time** _____ with each other.

8. Many psychologists believe **in** _____ carefully to their patients.

9. The students have been **looking forward to** _____ home over the winter break.

10. Nutritionists teach people to be careful **about** _____ the proper foods.

B. Together with a partner, read the following student writing and decide whether the verbs are correct as infinitives or gerunds.

Think Spring

I am always looking forward to have a long vacation with my family in the spring. I always choose the springtime because at that time all the leaves and flowers come back. What a beautiful season for people to spend time to travel! Especially with the weather so warm and mild, people spend time walk and enjoy the outdoors. You can see the sunshine on everyone's face. Everyone spends time to smile and relax. Also, people can wear beautiful lightweight clothing for traveling.   —Joanne Shao, College Student

C. Write some sentences about things you do during the different seasons. Use idiomatic expressions that take gerunds.

EXAMPLE   *In the spring I spend time fishing every weekend.*

_____

_____

_____

_____

_____

_____

_____

_____

_____

_____

_____

_____

_____

Verbs followed by infinitives

After some verbs, you must choose an infinitive instead of another verb form.

subject   +   verb + infinitive
Some students **need** to work part time.

Common Verbs Taking Infinitives		
agree	hope	pretend
ask	intend	promise
choose	manage	refuse
decide	need	seem
expect	offer	venture
fail	plan	want

Verbs followed by an object and the infinitive

You must use an object and then the infinitive to follow some verbs.

subject   +   verb   +   object   +   infinitive
Parents often **advise** <u>their children</u> to eat well.

Common Verbs Taking an Object + Infinitive			
advise	encourage	need	teach
allow	expect	permit	tell
ask	force	persuade	urge
convince	help	require	want

Writer's Alert

The verbs *make, let,* and *have* follow a different model. Use the infinitive without *to* (the base form).

subject + { *make* +   object + base form
{ *let*
{ *have*

She { **made**   me   <u>clean</u> my room.
{ **let**
{ **had**

Exercise 4

Look at the charts titled "Common Verbs Taking Infinitives" and "Common Verbs Taking an Object + Infinitive," and write sentences using some of these verbs. The topic is started with the first sentence.

1. (*agree*) *Married couples agree to make compromises.*
   _____

2. (*choose*) _____
   _____
   _____

3. (*expect*) _____
   _____
   _____

4. (*promise*) _____
   _____
   _____

5. (*allow*) _____
   _____
   _____

6. (*encourage*) _____
   _____
   _____

7. (*intend*) _____
   _____
   _____

8. (*help*) _____
   _____
   _____

9. (*plan*) _____

_____

_____

10. (*tell*) _____

_____

_____

Adjective expressions followed by infinitives

Use infinitives after certain adjectives.

subject + verb + adjective + infinitive

I	**am**	delighted	to know you.
It	**is**	easy	to understand the lesson.
They	**are**	pleased	to help.

Exercise 5

A. Finish the following sentences.

EXAMPLE   I am always **delighted** _to receive letters from home._

1. Teachers are **eager** _____

2. Parents are always **happy** _____

3. Friends are usually **delighted** _____

4. Spouses are often **willing** _____

5. Doctors are **anxious** _____

6. I am often **pleased** _____

7. It is sometimes **necessary** _____

8. It is often **impossible** _____

9. It is never too **late** _____

10. Good writing is **easy** _____

B. Write sentences using adjective expressions followed by infinitives.

1. _____
   _____

2. _____
   _____

3. _____
   _____

4. _____
   _____

5. _____
   _____

4
ger/inf

Summary Exercise

A. Read the following student writing, and fill in the correct form of the verb in parentheses by choosing gerunds, infinitives, or objects and infinitives.

Choosing a Major and Selecting a Profession

College students are always faced with the decision of (*choose*) _____ a major. For first-year students, of course, it is sometimes difficult (*decide*) _____ exactly which major they might want (*study*) _____. During the first two years of college, students must take required courses. After the sophomore year, however, students are asked (*declare*) _____ a major, and it is at this time that students begin (*specialize*) in the subject of their choosing. Thus, they need (*select*) _____ a major in a subject that interests them. Students must also consider (*find out*) _____ information about work in their field of interest. Advisors recommend (*experience*) _____ fieldwork in the student's area of interest, and in some colleges they expect students (*participate*) _____ in this activity as a required part of the curriculum. Once students have had experience in the field in which they intend (*work*) _____, they start (*understand*) _____ important facts about the professions they are choosing. They can also practice (*perform*) _____ the tasks of the particular profession. Students are greatly encouraged (*benefit*) _____ from on-the-job training. This experience lets students (*make*) _____ intelligent choices about their future careers.

4
ger/inf

B. Practice using the gerund and infinitive forms studied in this chapter. Working with a partner, answer the following questions by choosing the correct form of the verb.

1. When a person is studying a language, what is sometimes difficult? _____

   _____

   _____

2. During vacations, what do you enjoy? _____

   _____

   _____

3. Probably there are some things about the United States that bother you. Using verbs, name three things that you do not like.

_____

_____

_____

4. Probably there are some things about living in the United States that you prefer to living in your home country. Using verbs, name three.

_____

_____

_____

5. Using verbs, name three activities that are against the law in your country.

_____

_____

_____

4
ger/inf

6. When you are looking for a college, what should you consider doing first, second, and third? _____

_____

_____

7. What did your parents advise you to do before coming to this country?

_____

_____

_____

8. What do you recommend to others who might be coming to the United States?

_____

_____

_____

9. What do you appreciate about your life at this time?

_____

_____

_____

10. What three things do you hope to accomplish in the United States?

_____

_____

_____

C. Choose one of the questions from part b of the Summary Exercise, and freewrite about it. Notice your use of gerunds and infinitives.

_____

_____

_____

_____

_____

_____

_____

_____

_____

_____

_____

_____

_____

CHAPTER

5

Adjective Clauses

Adjective clauses (also called **relative clauses**) work like adjectives in complex sentences because they modify or add more information to nouns. You also can use them to combine simple sentences and form complex sentences, thus creating a more compact writing style.

In order to form a relative clause, use a relative pronoun: *who, whom, that, which,* or *whose. Who, whom, that,* and *whose* are used to modify people. *That, which,* and *whose* are used to modify animals, places and things. In spoken American English the use of *whom* generally is optional, but it is always used in formal writing.

5
clause

Writer's Alert

Where (place), *when* (time), and *why* (reason) are sometimes used to form adjective clauses.

PLACE   My hometown is a place **where** I long to be.

TIME   The late evening is the time **when** he writes a lot.

REASON   Safety is the reason **why** seat belts are required.

Place the relative clause as close as possible to the noun (the antecedent) that it modifies.

DRAFT   The <u>professor</u> is excellent **who teaches microbiology.**

REVISED   The <u>professor</u> **who teaches microbiology** is excellent.

The relative pronoun may be dropped from the sentence if it is not the subject of the adjective clause. Either form is correct.

INCLUDED   The apartment **that** we rented was very lovely.

OMITTED   The apartment we rented was very lovely.

Punctuation of adjective clauses

There are two kinds of adjective clauses: restrictive (necessary) and nonrestrictive (unnecessary).

Restrictive means that the sentence can be understood only if the adjective clause is included. The adjective clause is necessary for meaning. You don't need commas.

RESTRICTIVE CLAUSE (NECESSARY): NO COMMAS

People **who live in big cities** must walk their dogs on leashes.

Nonrestrictive means that the sentence can be understood without the adjective clause. The adjective clause is not necessary for meaning. You need commas.

NONRESTRICTIVE CLAUSE (UNNECESSARY): COMMAS

New York, **which has millions of inhabitants,** has strict laws about pets.

Writer's Alert

You use the relative pronoun *that* only when you have a restrictive adjective clause. *That* cannot be used to introduce nonrestrictive adjective clauses.

5
clause

Exercise 1

A. Read each sentence, and underline the adjective clause. Decide whether the clause is restrictive (necessary) or nonrestrictive (unnecessary) for meaning. If it is restrictive, use no commas; if it is nonrestrictive, use commas.

EXAMPLE ___R___ People who live in college dormitories sometimes have conflicts. (The clause is needed to understand the sentence more easily— do not use commas.)

___NR___ Penn State, which has designed sessions to help students in conflict, offers workshops for first-year students and during exams. (The clause is not needed to understand the sentence—use commas.)

1. _____ People who are living together are not necessarily going to get along well together.

2. _____ Students who come from so many diverse backgrounds experience problems.

3. _____ Many new college students who come from smaller families and are accustomed to living in their own space have not learned to live compatibly with others.

4. _____ Some colleges send questionnaires to students which discuss subjects like TV and study habits and attitudes toward budgets and guests.

5. _____ Colleges across the country have established dorms where students of similar educational and social interests can live together.

6. _____ "Theme houses" in which students with common interests live together are a growing trend on U.S. campuses.

7. _____ Dormitories where students are immersed in a foreign language have existed for many years.

8. _____ The California State University campus which is in Long Beach California offers an International House dormitory.

9. _____ In the International House where many foreign students and Americans live students exchange language and culture.

10. _____ In addition, dormitories that focus on such themes as fields of study, health, and spirituality are being established.

B. Write two sentences with restrictive adjective clauses and two sentences with nonrestrictive adjective clauses. Give them to a partner to punctuate correctly.

_____

_____

_____

_____

_____

_____

_____

_____

_____

_____

Subject pronouns

Use *who, that,* or *which* to replace a **subject pronoun** with a relative clause.

SIMPLE SENTENCE   Mahatma Gandhi led India to independence.

                     subject pronoun
SIMPLE SENTENCE   **He** was called the father of modern India.

COMBINED   Mahatma Gandhi, **who** was called the father of modern India, led India to independence.

Exercise 2

A. In each pair of sentences, replace the underlined subject pronoun or repeated noun in the second sentence with *who, which* or *that* to form an adjective clause. Combine the two sentences to form a complex sentence. Punctuate as necessary.

EXAMPLE   There are many well-known men. They are leaders of Native American tribes.

There are many well-known men who are leaders of Native American Indian tribes.

1. Native American groups represent an important part of U.S. history. They have distinct languages and cultures.

   _____

   _____

2. Geronimo was an Apache leader. He was born in 1829 and died in 1909.

   _____

   _____

3. He was called Goyathlay. This means "one who yawns" in Apache. _____

   _____

   _____

4. Geronimo conducted many raids against both Mexican and American settlements in the Southwest. He wanted to defend his people against white encroachment on Apach land. _____

   _____

   _____

5. History remembers another great tribe. It was called the Cheyenne. _____

   _____

   _____

6. The Cheyenne were great warriors. They called their leader Chief Wolf Robe.

   _____

   _____

7. The Cheyenne were famous hunters. <u>They</u> lived on the Great Plains. _____

_____

_____

8. They later settled on the Cheyenne River of North Dakota. <u>It</u> is named after the

Cheyenne tribe. _____

_____

_____

9. The Cheyenne and other tribes formed an alliance. <u>They</u> later helped to defeat General

George Custer at the Battle of the Little Bighorn. _____

_____

_____

10. These people witnessed the disappearance of both the buffalo and the wild frontier

during their lifetimes. <u>They</u> were from various tribes. _____

_____

_____

B. Write three sentences of your own with adjective clauses similar to those in Exercise
2a. Give them to a partner to punctuate correctly.

_____

_____

_____

_____

_____

Object pronouns

Use *who, whom, that,* or *which* to replace an **object pronoun** with a relative clause.

SIMPLE SENTENCE   Gandhi was a political and spiritual leader.

                                        object pronoun
SIMPLE SENTENCE   People admired **him.**

COMBINED   Gandhi was a political and spiritual leader **whom** people admired.

Exercise 3

A. In each pair of sentences, replace the underlined object pronoun or a repeated noun in the second sentence with *who, whom, which,* or *that* to form an adjective clause. Combine the two sentences to form a complex sentence. Punctuate as necessary.

EXAMPLE   Manifest Destiny is a term. We use it to describe the expansion of the U.S. territories in the West.

Manifest Destiny is a term that we use to describe the expansion of the U.S. territories in the West.

1. In the 1800s many Americans were looking for a new life. They believed it could be found in the lands of the West. _____

_____

_____

2. Many Americans wanted the chance to own land. They desired it for farming.

_____

_____

3. By 1830, some lands in Mexico were settled by twenty thousand new people. The Mexican government considered them Mexican. _____

_____

_____

4. These new settlers continued to farm the lands of the Mexican territories. The Mexican government tried to control these new settlers. _____

_____

_____

5. Stephen Austin went to Mexico City to discuss the problem. The Mexicans threw him into prison. _____

_____

_____

6. The new Texans revolted against the Mexican government and took over a fort. A Mexican general later tried to rescue it._____

_____

_____

7. The Texans won the battle and defeated the Mexican general. He was then held captive. _____

_____

_____

8. The Texans won independence from the Mexican government. They didn't want to obey the Mexican government._____

_____

_____

9. Texas became an independent nation. Its citizens called it the Lone Star State.

_____

_____

10. Sam Houston became the first president of Texas. People remember him for his brave leadership. _____

_____

_____

B. Write three sentences of your own with adjective clauses similar to those in Exercise 3a. Give them to a partner to punctuate correctly.

_____

_____

_____

Possessive pronouns

Use *whose* to replace a **possessive pronoun** with a relative clause.

SIMPLE SENTENCE He was a great leader.

                                    possessive pronoun
SIMPLE SENTENCE People appreciated **his** simple way of life.

COMBINED He was a great leader **whose** simple way of life people appreciated.

Name: _____ Date: _____

Exercise 4

A. In the second sentence of each pair, replace the underlined possessive pronoun with *whose* to form an adjective clause. Combine the two sentences to form a complex sentence. Punctuate as necessary.

EXAMPLE   There were many different Native American groups. We can appreciate their rich heritage today.

There were many different Native American groups whose rich heritage we
can appreciate today.

1. The Sioux are a group of Native Americans. Their language is spoken in various dialects across the United States. _____

   _____

2. Sitting Bull was a great Sioux leader. His wisdom, bravery, and powers of healing are legendary. _____

   _____

3. In order to fight off hostile U.S. troops, Sitting Bull participated in a great battle. Its name—the Battle of the Little Bighorn—is still famous today. _____

   _____

4. The Iroquois Nation is a union of Iroquois-speaking Native Americans. Its tribes include the Seneca, Cayuga, Onondaga, Oneida, and Mohawk. _____

   _____

5. The union has an organization called the Grand Council. Its aim is both to unite individual members and to maintain autonomy for each tribe. _____

   _____

6. The Iroquois are remembered for the political organization of the Iroquois Nation. Its democratic principles may have influenced the writing of the U.S. Constitution.

   _____

   _____

7. Today the Navajo constitute the largest Native American tribe left in the United States. <u>Their</u> numbers exceed 150,000. _____

_____

8. The Navajo have the best-preserved Native American culture in North America. <u>Their</u> traditional view of the world includes belief in both good and evil forces. _____

_____

9. The Navajo artists create sand paintings. <u>Their</u> symbolic powers are believed to cure sick people. _____

_____

10. A photographer preserved the heritage and immortalized the culture of Native Americans. <u>His</u> name was Edward S. Curtis. _____

_____

B. Write three sentences of your own with adjective clauses similar to those in Exercise 4a. Give them to a partner to punctuate correctly.

_____

_____

_____

_____

_____

_____

Object of a preposition

Use a preposition plus *who, whom, which,* or *whose* to replace the **object of a preposition** with a relative clause.

SIMPLE SENTENCE Gandhi believed in the independence of India.

object of preposition
SIMPLE SENTENCE He worked tirelessly **for it.**

COMBINED Gandhi believed in the independence of India, **for which** he worked tirelessly.

Exercise 5

A. In each pair of sentences, replace the underlined object of a preposition or a repeated noun in the second sentence with *who, whom, which,* or *whose* to form an adjective clause. Combine the two sentences to form a complex sentence. Punctuate as necessary. Use either of the two possible forms.

EXAMPLE   In the 1800s Edward S. Curtis photographed many different Native Americans. People were interested **in** them.

FORMAL   In the 1800s Edward S. Curtis photographed many different Native Americans, **in whom** people were interested.

INFORMAL   In the 1800s Edward S. Curtis photographed many different Native Americans, **whom** people were interested **in.**

1. Edward S. Curtis is famous for his photographs of Native Americans. There was great curiosity **about** them in both the United States and Europe. _____

_____

_____

2. Curtis and others took many photographs. Native Americans were often resistant **to** these photographs. _____

_____

_____

3. Government officials wanted to document the Native Americans. They had great interest **about** their lives. _____

_____

_____

4. Many photographers were interested in taking historical photographs. They traveled all over the West **for** them. _____

_____

_____

5. The photographers were busy taking historical photographs. Some Native Americans were willing to cooperate **with** these photographers. _____

_____

_____

6. Curtis documented the Native American culture quite accurately. He received a lot of praise **for** this. _____

_____

_____

7. The pictures educated people about the Native American way of life. Viewers began to have a greater respect **for** it. _____

_____

_____

8. During this period the Native Americans were seen as a threatened race. Other people began to have great sympathy **for** them. _____

_____

_____

9. Without the photographs taken at this time, we would have lost much of the Native American heritage. We have learned so many things **from** it. _____

_____

_____

10. The photographs of Native Americans leave a rich legacy. We are grateful **for** this rich legacy. _____

_____

_____

B. Write three sentences of your own with adjective clauses similar to those in Exercise 5a. Give them to a partner to punctuate correctly.

_____

_____

_____

_____

_____

_____

Object of a quantifier

Use a quantifier plus *who, whom, which,* or *whose* to replace the *object of a quantifier* with a relative clause.

SIMPLE SENTENCE Gandhi also worked for equality for all people in India.

object of quantifier
SIMPLE SENTENCE **Many of them** were very poor.

COMBINED Gandhi also worked for equality for all people in India, **many of whom** were very poor.

Exercise 6

A. In the second sentence of each pair, replace the underlined pronoun or a repeated noun that is the object of a quantifier with *who, whom, which,* or *whose* to form an adjective clause. Combine the two sentences to form a complex sentence. Punctuate as necessary.

EXAMPLE   There are many different groups of immigrants in the United States. **Some of** them came from European countries.

There are many different groups of immigrants in the United States, some

of whom came from European countries.

1. The early English immigrants were looking for a new way of life. **The first of** them settled in Jamestown, Virginia, and in Plymouth, Massachusetts. _____

    _____

    _____

2. In the late 1600s, large numbers of immigrants were Germans. Many of them settled in Pennsylvania. _____

    _____

3. Scotch-Irish immigrants came to America in large numbers. **Most of** them settled in lands along the frontier. _____

    _____

    _____

4. French Huguenots came to the New World to flee religious persecution. **Some of** them settled in New York State. _____

    _____

    _____

5. People from many different nations came to America for a new life. **Each of** them brought their own customs and ideas. _____

    _____

6. The early settlers struggled to survive. **The majority of** them were farmers.

    _____

7. The colonists also lived in manufacturing towns, such as Philadelphia, New York, Boston, Newport, and Charleston. **Many of** <u>them</u> were already skilled workers.

_____

_____

8. The early settlers had large families. **Most of** <u>their</u> children were needed to help work.

_____

9. Education was not always available to the early settlers. **Few of** <u>them</u> were ever formally educated. _____

_____

10. People came to America looking for rights. **Most of** <u>these rights</u> were religious, social, and civil freedoms._____

_____

_____

 B. Write three sentences of your own with adjective clauses similar to those in Exercise 6a. Give them to a partner to punctuate correctly.

_____

_____

Adjective clauses changed to phrases

Adjective clauses can be changed to **adjective phrases** when the relative pronoun is the subject of the adjective clause. To change a clause with a *be* verb to a phrase, omit the relative pronoun and the *be* verb.

CLAUSE (WITH *BE*)   He is the man **<u>who is</u> studying German.**

PHRASE   He is the man **studying German.**

To change a clause with another verb to a phrase, omit the relative pronoun and change the verb to the present participle form.

CLAUSE (WITHOUT *BE*)   He is the man **who <u>wants</u> to study German.**

PHRASE   He is the man **<u>wanting</u> to study German.**

Exercise 7

A. Read each sentence, and underline the adjective clause. Change the clause to a phrase, following the rules above.

EXAMPLE   Great structures ~~which were~~ built many centuries ago represent great ancient cultures.

1. The Egyptian pyramids, which were built for the great pharaohs, were used as royal tombs.

2. The thousands of workers who were needed to build these mysterious monuments were simple peasants.

3. The technical perfection that was achieved by Egyptian architects makes these pyramids one of the world's great wonders.

4. Ancient cultures which originated in Central and South America and in Mexico built pyramids as temples.

5. One huge pyramid which still stands near Mexico City is about fifty-four meters high.

6. The Pyramid of the Sun, which is located in central Mexico, is an outstanding architectural achievement.

7. Panels of hieroglyphics that ornament the inside of the temple are of great historical interest.

8. The pyramids, which remind us of the great wisdom of ancient peoples, remain a mystery.

B. Look back at Exercises 1, 2, and 3 in this chapter. With a partner, decide whether some of the adjective clauses can be changed into adjective phrases. Make the necessary changes.

5
clause

Summary Exercise

A. Working with another student, read the following passage and underline the adjective clauses. Punctuate as necessary. The first sentence is done for you.

Con-Son, A Beautiful Island of Vietnam

Vietnam, <u>which is a small country in Southeast Asia</u>, is shaped like the letter *S*. With a long stretch of seashore on the Pacific Ocean, it has many beautiful beaches and islands. One of the most beautiful and important islands is Con-Son.

Con-Son is located southwest of Saigon which is the capital of Vietnam. Forty miles away from the shore, Con-Son is surrounded by clear water and fine sand beaches. There is an abundance of coconut trees that were planted by prisoners who were kept there in the eighteenth century. Visitors who wish to experience this wonderful tropical island can come by plane or boat. Visitors who come by boat will have a chance to see a spectacular tunnel gate whose shape is formed by thousands of coconut trees and wildflowers. After traveling through this natural gate, the boat docks at Bai-Dam beach where passengers can look through the light blue water and see a large array of fish that are dancing in the sea.

On top of a mountain on the island there is a lighthouse that was built by the French government when Vietnam was a French colony. During the war between the South and the North of the country, Con-Son was an island to which political prisoners were sent. Some have chosen to stay on as residents of this magical island. The sounds of coconut leaves that move in the air and waves that hit the shore make Con-Son a tropical paradise.

—Phat V. Phung, College Student

B. Read the following passage, and fill in the correct relative pronouns. Punctuate as needed. The first sentence is done for you.

Eleanor Roosevelt, An Outstanding First Lady

Eleanor Roosevelt, ____*who*____ was the wife of Franklin D. Roosevelt, the thirty-second president of the United States, was born on October 11, 1884, and died on November 7, 1962. Eleanor Roosevelt _____ was one of the most active first ladies of the twentieth century was a strong advocate of humanitarian causes _____

5
clause

included employment of youth and civil rights for African Americans and women. In 1905 Eleanor married Franklin _____ was her cousin. They had six children, one of _____ died as an infant.

Eleanor Roosevelt _____ is remembered as a highly gifted and energetic woman expanded the role of first lady _____ was traditionally limited. She was a tireless advocate for the underprivileged and for minorities. Eleanor _____ was one of the most outspoken women in American public life worked to improve education and international understanding. Throughout her life Eleanor continued to fight for the human rights in _____ she so strongly believed. The United Nations *Declaration of Human Rights* _____ promised a dignified and secure future for all people was adopted on December 10, 1948, in large part because of the personal and political vision of Eleanor Roosevelt _____ was the U.S. representative to the UN at that time.

Eleanor Roosevelt was an extraordinarily active first lady during _____ lifetime many important achievements were made for a better world.

C. Choose one of the following topics, and develop a paragraph. Use adjective clauses to make your writing more descriptive.

An important political figure or political event from your country

Your country

A celebrity you admire

Home

_____

_____

_____

_____

_____

_____

_____

_____

_____

_____

_____

_____

_____

_____

_____

_____

_____

 D. Choose a paper in progress, and look for adjective clauses or phrases. Add these structures to your writing to make it more effective.

Adverb Clauses

Adverb clauses work like adverbs in complex sentences because they modify or add more information to verbs.

Adverb clauses of time, reason, contrast, and condition

Adverb clauses give information about time, reason, contrast, and condition.

Some Words to Introduce Adverb Clauses				
TIME		**REASON**	**CONTRAST**	**CONDITION**
while	when	because	although	if
before	whenever	since	though	even if
since	as soon as	as	even though	only if
until	after	now that	while	unless
once	as		whereas	provided that
				as long as

TIME	<u>**When** the weather changes</u>, people tend to catch the flu.
	Senior citizens choose to get flu shots <u>**before** they get sick.</u>
REASON	<u>**Since** the weather has turned colder</u>, many people have gotten sick.
	It is difficult to get an appointment at the doctor's office <u>**because** flu season has started.</u>
CONTRAST	<u>**Although** some people choose to get flu shots</u>, others do not.
	Some people choose to get flu shots <u>**while** others do not.</u>
CONDITION	<u>**If** you are unaccustomed to winter weather</u>, you can get an inoculation to protect yourself.
	You may catch the flu <u>**unless** you dress in warm clothes.</u>

Punctuation of adverb clauses

An adverb clause that is placed at the beginning of a sentence must be followed by a comma. Notice the punctuation of the adverb clauses in the previous examples and in those that following.

When foreign students try to communicate with a native English speaker, they improve their language skills more easily.

Foreign students should set definite goals for themselves **if they want to learn English more efficiently.**

Name: _____ Date: _____

Exercise 1

A. Using the rules about punctuation of adverb clauses, read the following sentences, underline the adverb clauses, and punctuate as necessary.

1. The number of foreign students studying in the United States is steadily increasing because studying abroad gives them many new life experiences.

2. This experience can present many dilemmas for students as they are challenged by speaking and studying in a new language.

3. When students first start to speak in English they often feel uncomfortable and inhibited.

4. Since the difficulties of communicating in a second language can be daunting foreign students sometimes choose to spend time with those who speak their own language.

5. However, if foreign students wish to improve their English they should try not only socializing with native English speakers but also joining in the activities of a school club.

B. Read the following paragraph. Underline adverb clauses, and punctuate as needed.

Americans Should Buy American

Since I came to the United States I have often noticed that there are many Japanese cars in this country. It would be a better idea for Americans to buy cars made in America because this would solve the growing problem of unemployment in the country, and it might even improve the balance of trade between Japan and the United States. When American car manufacturers began to produce smaller, better designed, better built, and more economical cars a few years ago it became practical for American consumers to buy American automobiles. As soon as American people begin to realize the importance of buying American products they will help the country's economic problems and maybe even improve relations between Japan and the United States as well.

Yuka Yashiro, College Student

Using adverb clauses

Writers can use adverb clauses to express time, reason, contrast and condition. It is necessary to choose the appropriate subordinator when you create these clauses.

Name: _____ Date: _____

Exercise 2

A. Combine the following sentences, using the subordinator in parentheses to create an adverb clause to express *time*. Circle the subordinator. Punctuate as necessary.

EXAMPLE   I travel back home. I take the bus. (*when*)

(When) I travel back home, I take the bus. _____

1. I leave New York City. I go directly to the subway station. (*whenever*) _____
   _____
   _____

2. I get to the subway station. I take the No. 1 train downtown. (*after*) _____
   _____
   _____

3. I get off the subway car. It gets to the 42nd Street stop. (*as soon as*) _____
   _____
   _____

4. I get off at the 42nd Street subway station. I follow the signs to the Port Authority bus station. (*after*) _____
   _____
   _____

5. I arrive at the Port Authority. I go to the Adirondack Trailways desk to buy a round-trip ticket to upstate New York. (*when*) _____
   _____
   _____

6. I purchase my round trip ticket. I go downstairs to gate 33. (*once*) _____
   _____
   _____

7. I make certain the bus is going to my town. I get on it. (*before*) _____
   _____
   _____

6
clause

8. The bus pulls into the station in my hometown. I see my parents waiting for me. (*as soon as*) _____

_____

_____

B. Combine the following sentences by using the subordinator in parentheses to create an adverb clause expressing *reason*. Circle the subordinator. Punctuate as necessary.

EXAMPLE   The weather has gotten very cold. Simple things have become difficult (*since*)

(Since) the weather has gotten very cold, simple things have become difficult.

1. The temperature dropped to frigid levels. Many problems have resulted. (*because*)

_____

_____

2. The weather has gone way below the freezing point. Everyone must dress in many layers of clothing and must always wear a hat and gloves. (*since*) _____

_____

3. Weather advisories are issued. People need to exercise extreme caution on the roads. (*because*) _____

_____

4. Motorists must leave for work an hour early. The roads have become very icy. (*because*)

_____

_____

5. Some schools have been closed. Their heating systems have been malfunctioning. (*because*) _____

_____

_____

6. The grocery stores have often been crowded with customers. People have begun buying extra food in case of a snowstorm. (*since*) _____

_____

_____

7. Utility companies are asking people to reduce their energy use. The frigid temperatures are raising demand for electricity. (*because*) _____

_____

_____

8. Traveling has become difficult. The winter weather has arrived. (*since*) _____

_____

_____

C. Combine the following sentences, using the subordinator in parentheses to create an adverb clause expressing *contrast*. Circle the subordinator. Punctuate as necessary.

EXAMPLE Languages are fun to learn. They can also be unpredictable. (although)

(Although) languages are fun to learn, they can also be unpredictable.

1. Many people study the English language. It is not the most widely spoken language in the world. (*though*) _____

_____

2. Mandarin Chinese is the most widely spoken language in the world. Many people choose to learn English instead. (*although*) _____

_____

_____

3. In Switzerland four languages are spoken. The official language is French. (*although*)

_____

_____

4. In Somalia only one language is spoken. More than a thousand different languages are spoken on the African continent. (*whereas*) _____

_____

5. In the United States we say that the toilet is in the bathroom. In England it is in the water closet. (*but*) _____

_____

6. In Australia fried potatoes are called chips. In the United States they are called french fries. (*whereas*) _____

_____

7. Esperanto is no longer a widely used language. It is spoken by some eight million people. (*while*) _____

_____

8. Germany has only one official language, called High German. There are numerous dialects throughout the country. (*although*) _____

_____

D. Combine the following sentences, using the subordinator in parentheses to create an adverb clause expressing *condition*. Circle the subordinator. Punctuate as necessary.

EXAMPLE   You need to understand body language. You want to assimilate easily into a new culture. (*if*)

You need to understand body language (if) you want to assimilate easily into a new culture.

1. In some cultures you are considered rude. You look directly into the eyes of another person while talking. (*if*) _____

_____

2. In American culture you are considered rude. You do not look into the eyes of a person while talking. (*if*) _____

_____

3. In some cultures you are easily accepted when you are visiting. You remove your shoes when you are inside the home. (*provided that*) _____

_____

4. In American culture you don't need to remove shoes in the home. You are visiting. (*provided*) _____

_____

5. In some Hispanic cultures people stand very close to one another in conversation. They wish to communicate friendship. (*if*) _____

_____

6. You maintain enough physical distance between yourself and a person you are talking to. In American culture people feel more comfortable. (*as long as*) _____

_____

7. In certain countries either a handshake or a bow is expected. People are meeting formally. (*if*) _____

_____

8. People need to learn unspoken behaviors of a new culture. They know the language. (*even if*) _____

_____

6
clause

Name: _____ Date: _____

Summary Exercise

A. Finish each of the following sentences, using a subordinator of time, reason, contrast, or condition, as indicated in brackets.

1. Traveling can teach you many wonderful things _____
   _____ [reason]

2. You have the opportunity to know your own country better _____
   _____ [time]

3. The experience can teach you about yourself _____
   _____ [condition]

4. There are often many surprises _____
   _____ [time]

5. _____
   _____ it's great to get back home. [contrast]

B. Write four sentences of your own, using each type of adverb clause. Exchange sentences with a partner, and discuss meaning and punctuation.

_____

_____

_____

_____

_____

_____

_____

_____

C. Fill in the blank with a correct word or words to introduce the adverb clause. Notice the punctuation.

Learning Japanese as a Second Language

_____ we sat aboard a plane headed for Japan, my son and I began to study our *Speedy Japanese* book for beginners. We wanted to learn the numbers 1 to 10 in Japanese _____ we landed _____ we believed that this knowledge would help us _____ we arrived.

_____ we made our way through the crowded airport, the new sound of the language was strange and exciting. _____ we saw our friend who was waiting for us, we felt more relaxed. She helped to translate signs for us and helped us to maneuver in this wonderful new country. _____ we got to her apartment, we wanted to sleep, _____ it was only 6 p.m.

The Japanese people were so patient and so friendly to us _____ we met them. _____ we needed help of any kind, they were always willing to give it. _____ we were feeling rather homesick, we went to a baseball game. It felt so good to see that familiar sport, _____ the Japanese version of the game is a little different.

_____ spending a whole month in a new country, we felt almost strange arriving back at Kennedy Airport in New York. We had grown accustomed to hearing a language that we couldn't understand, _____ back in New York we suddenly were a part of the system. This is an experience you cannot fully understand _____ you have traveled to a foreign land. We learned that _____ we wanted to continue our study of Japan and the Japanese people, we would have to return for many more months.

D. Choose one of the topics below, and develop a short paragraph. Use adverb clauses to express time, reason, contrast, or condition.

A trip back home
How the weather affects your life
Something that has surprised you about the United States
An unusual experience learning a new language

_____

_____

_____

_____

_____

_____

_____

_____

_____

_____

_____

_____

_____

_____

 E. Choose a paper in progress, and look for adverb clauses. Add these structures to your writing to make it more effective.

Noun Clauses

When you combine the three types of **noun clauses** with other sentence parts to form complex sentences, these clauses work like nouns in the sentences.

THAT CLAUSE   I believe **that** <u>life exists in other solar systems.</u>

YES/NO QUESTION I wonder **if** <u>life exists in other solar systems.</u>
CLAUSE
                I wonder **whether** <u>life exists in other solar systems.</u>

WH- QUESTION   I wonder **where** <u>signs of other life may be found.</u>
CLAUSE

This third kind of noun clause is formed by a question that is embedded into the sentence as a statement. It is introduced by a question word such as *who, whom, what, where, when, which, why, how, how much,* or *how many.* Sometimes the noun clause follows an introductory clause, and then the word order of the noun clause does not change. It remains the same as the word order in the original question. Note how this works.

QUESTION   Who discovered the fire?

NOUN CLAUSE   Do you know **who discovered the fire?**

QUESTION   What started the fire?

NOUN CLAUSE   Did anyone see **what started the fire?**

QUESTION   How much damage was caused?

NOUN CLAUSE   The company knows **how much damage was caused.**

QUESTION   Which fire fighters came to help?

NOUN CLAUSE   He knows **which fire fighters came to help.**

Name: _____. Date: _____

Exercise 1

A. Underline the noun clauses in the following sentences.

EXAMPLE   Scientists know <u>that the sun is just one of millions of stars</u>.

1. It is a fact that there are many solar systems in the Milky Way.

2. How many other solar systems exist beyond our solar system is unknown.

3. It is also not known whether there is any form of life in these other solar systems.

4. Scientists continue to investigate how the universe began.

5. Many people believe that the universe is expanding; others think that it is contracting.

6. The big bang theory states that the universe began to expand from a single point billions of years ago.

7. Some versions of the theory suggest that many universes may have come into existence in much the same way.

8. It is also believed, however, that many galaxies are obscured from view.

9. Many people wonder, in fact, whether the number of galaxies may be infinite.

10. Because there may be millions of other solar systems in the universe, many people think that life must exist elsewhere.

B. Read the following paragraph, and underline the noun clauses.

The Importance of Work

It is true that people need to work for many reasons and that they can profit from the experience. Work has taught me how to be assertive, how to be responsible, and how to be punctual. Having a job taught me that it is important to be able to communicate with superiors and other workers. Formerly, I did not know how to get along well with others, but my work experience taught me this important lesson. That people work well together in any job is very necessary. I also learned that I had a responsiblity to others and not just to myself. It was important that I arrive at work on time and that I put forth my best effort. What I learned from my work experience has been invaluable in teaching me life lessons.

—Albina Kohlman, College Student

Word order changes in *wh-* question clauses

Writer's Alert

The word order of a *wh-* question noun clause may vary. Note how this works.

- The word order changes when the question includes a form of *be* and a subject complement.

  QUESTION   Who **are** your friends?

  NOUN CLAUSE   I wonder who your friends **are.**

- The word order changes when the question includes a modal.

  QUESTION   How **can** I meet them?

  NOUN CLAUSE   Please tell me how I **can** meet them.

- The word order changes when the question includes the auxiliary *do, does,* or *did.*

  QUESTION   When **do** you plan to introduce us?

  NOUN CLAUSE   Let me know when you plan to introduce us.

- The word order changes when the question includes the auxiliary *have, has,* or *had.*

  QUESTION   How **have** you met so many people?

  NOUN CLAUSE   I'm interested in how you **have** met so many people.

7
clause

Exercise 2

A. Change the following questions into noun clauses by embedding them into sentences as both subjects and objects. Remember that the word order of the question sometimes changes in the noun clause.

EXAMPLE   What did the president say in last night's speech?

SUBJECT   **What the president said in last night's speech** is in the newspaper.

OBJECT   I read **what the president said in last night's speech** in the newspaper.

1. Who is in the audience?

   _____ doesn't interest me.

   The television shows us _____.

2. Where are the secret service agents?

   _____ is difficult to see.

   It is difficult to see _____.

3. Where can I meet the president?

   _____ is still unknown.

   It is still not known _____.

4. When do you plan to introduce us?

   _____ is very important to me.

   It is very important to me _____.

5. How has the president become so popular?

   _____ is of great interest to me.

   I am greatly interested in _____.

B. Write questions to ask another classmate about some event he or she has seen, such as a concert, a movie, or a political event. Report the information you receive, and underline the noun clauses you write. Remember that the word order sometimes changes.

QUESTION   Who was performing at the concert?

REPORT   *My classmate knows who was performing at the concert. My classmate said that the band is called the Gypsy Kings.*

C. Combine the following sentences by using noun clauses to form *that* clauses.

EXAMPLE   The sun is ninety-three million miles from the earth. Scientists know it.

COMBINED   *Scientists know that the sun is ninety-three million miles from the earth.*

1. Space exploration has advantages and disadvantages. Everyone realizes this.

   _____

   _____

2. The cost of space exploration is very high. The benefits are also high. It is understood.

   _____

   _____

3. We have the technological know-how to develop rockets. It is amazing. _____

   _____

4. To be able to leave the earth's atmosphere and travel into space is an extraordinary accomplishment. It cannot be denied. _____

   _____

5. People have always had a great interest in learning about the universe. It is easily understood. _____

   _____

6. The Greek astronomer Eratosthenes measured the earth's size fairly accurately. It is a fact. _____

   _____

7. The earth orbits the sun. Copernicus was the first modern European to theorize this.

   _____

   _____

8. Pluto has one moon. In 1978 scientists discovered this fact. _____

   _____

9. The two nearest galaxies are the Andromeda galaxy and the Magellanic Clouds. We now know this. _____

   _____

7
clause

10. People will always try to explore the unknown territories of both the planet and the sky above. It is true. _____

_____

_____

Summary Exercise

A. Do you believe that there is life on other planets or in other solar systems? Discuss your thoughts and beliefs in a short paragraph. Use all three kinds of noun clauses in your writing. Use expressions such as *I believe that, I wonder if/whether, I think that,* and *it is a fact that.* Underline all noun clauses.

_____

_____

_____

_____

_____

_____

_____

_____

_____

_____

_____

_____

_____

B. Write about the value of work in your life. Include noun clauses to make your writing more effective.

_____

_____

_____

_____

_____

_____

_____

_____

7
clause

_____

_____

_____

_____

_____

_____

_____

_____

 C. Read a paper in progress and underline all the noun clauses you see, or edit your paper by creating noun clauses where they might be effective.

Summary exercise for adjective, adverb, and noun clauses

Revise the following paragraphs by combining the sentences in brackets. You will form adjective, adverb, or noun clauses to improve the writing. Punctuate as needed.

Albert Einstein

[Albert Einstein contributed more than any other scientist to the world of the twentieth century. He was born in Germany in 1879 and died in the United States in 1955.] [Einstein actually failed school examinations. This happened when he was very young.] [This is an interesting fact. He graduated in 1900 as a teacher of mathematics and physics.]

[Einstein wrote three important papers on the subject of physics. One of these papers was about quantum mechanics. Quantum mechanics is a theory of physics concerned with electrons and light.] [The second paper proposed the theory of relativity. In this paper Einstein presented new and important ideas about energy and mass.] [The third paper considered atomic motion. The paper involved statistical mechanics.]

[Einstein's theory of relativity was a new way of looking at time, space, matter, and energy. He is most remembered for this theory.] [A small amount of matter can produce a large amount of energy. He proved this.] [Einstein left the world with many new theories of physics. He won the Nobel Price for Physics in 1921 for these theories.] [There is a fundamental order to all of nature and there is a unity of all humanity. He belived this.] For these reasons Einstein worked throughout his life to spread knowledge and world peace.

7
clause

USING VERBS

Simple Present and Simple Past Tense

The third person -*s* or -*es* ending

The present tense verbs in English are easy to write, but you must remember to add an -*s* or -*es* to verbs that are third person singular.

Subject	Verb	Subject	Verb + -*s*
I		he	
you (sing., pl.)		she	
we	write	it (an animal,	writes
they		a thing,	
		a concept)	

Subjects and verbs

Check the following points to make sure that your present tense verbs are correct when you edit your writing.

- Check the subject and the verb in a simple sentence.

  NOT APPROPRIATE The hummingbird gather nectar from flowers.

  subject   verb

  CORRECT   The **hummingbird gathers** nectar from flowers.

- Check whether the subject and the verb are separated by phrases.

  NOT APPROPRIATE The hummingbird of those regions gather nectar.

	subject	verb

CORRECT   The **hummingbird** of those regions **gathers** nectar.
Hummingbird, not *regions,* is the subject.

- Check for compound verbs (more than one verb) in a simple sentence.

NOT APPROPRIATE The hummingbird visit our garden, gather nectar, and leave quietly.

CORRECT   The **hummingbird visits** our garden, **gathers** nectar, and **leaves** quietly.

- Check for agreement between the subject and the verb in a complex sentence (see 14d-1).

NOT APPROPRIATE When the **snow fall,** we enjoy the scenery.

CORRECT   When the **snow falls,** we enjoy the scenery.

NOT APPROPRIATE The young **man** that I work with **live** in town.

CORRECT   The young **man** that I work with **lives** in town.

Writer's Alert

Sometimes you need to be careful to match the *-s* and *-es* endings of verbs in the main clause and in the adjective clause.

The young **man** that **works** with me **lives** in town.

- Check for correct use of the auxiliary *do, don't, does,* and *doesn't.*

NOT APPROPRIATE That restaurant do give special discount dinners.

CORRECT   That restaurant **does** give special discount dinners.

- Check for correct use of modal auxiliaries.

NOT APPROPRIATE The president might gives a speech this evening.

CORRECT   The president **might give** a speech this evening.

Exercise 1

A. Read the following sentences, and write the correct present tense form of the verb in the blank.

EXAMPLE   An English language class sometimes _____*feels*_____ (*feel*) like a United Nations.

1. Our classmates (*come*) _____ from five different countries.

2. Some students (*originate*) _____ from Japan, China, and Korea.

3. Another student (*represent*) _____ her country, Egypt.

4. Two other students (*come*) _____ from Mexico.

5. Many students (*hope*) _____ to graduate from a U.S. university.

6. Multinational students (*communicate*) _____ with each other in the language they have in common, English.

7. An English as a Second Language class (*teach*) _____ everyone that the world is multilingual and multicultural.

B. Read the following sentences, and check the subjects and verbs. Add -*s* or -*es* to the underline verbs if needed.

EXAMPLE   Sound travel ___*S*___ through the air at approximately 1,100 feet per second.

1. Invisible vibrations make_____ sound.

2. Sound is made by the vibration of objects, which send_____ waves through the air.

3. The number of the vibrations make_____ a difference; it determine_____ the kind of sound we hear_____.

4. Sounds can_____ be low, high, soft, or loud.

5. If an object vibrate_____ many times per second, it make_____ a high-frequency sound.

8
verb

6. High frequencies make_____ high-pitched sounds.

7. Objects that vibrate_____ very slowly produce_____ low-frequency waves and make_____ low-pitched sounds.

8. However, sound do_____ travel very well under water.

9. Many creatures of the ocean perceive_____ the vibrations of sound from great distances.

10. Sound can_____ travel_____ more slowly than light; therefore, during electrical storms, the sound of the thunder take_____ longer to reach us than the sight of the lightning do_____.

C. Write the following types of sentences, using the third person singular. Exchange sentences with a partner to edit for third person -s. When you have both finished editing, go over the sentences together to see if you agree on the verb endings.

1. Write a simple sentence.

_____

_____

2. Write a sentence with a subject and verb separated by a phrase.

_____

_____

3. Write a sentence with compound verbs.

_____

_____

4. Write a complex sentence.

_____

_____

5. Write a sentence using the auxiliary *do* or *does* or using the negative.

_____

_____

6. Write a sentence using a modal.

_____

_____

Simple present and simple past

These are the two tenses that add no helping verbs to form the verb. No other verb forms can stand alone!

SIMPLE PRESENT   They **live** in the dormitory this semester.

SIMPLE PAST   They **lived** in an apartment last semester.

NOT APPROPRIATE   The student **studying** in the library yesterday.
    The writer uses the present participle without any helping verb. In English this is not possible.

CORRECT   The student **was studying** in the library yesterday.
    Now the verb form is a completed verb phrase with a helping verb and a verb form.

8
verb

Exercise 2

A. If the verb in parentheses in each of the following sentences is in a completed form of simple present or simple past tense, write *correct* on the line. If the verb is incomplete, change it to either simple present or simple past tense and rewrite the sentence.

EXAMPLE   Some Americans (*choosing*) to educate their children at home.

Some Americans choose to educate their children at home.

1. Home schooling (*began*) in the 1960s.

    _____

2. Today many people (*believing*) in home schooling.

    _____

3. Home schooling (*offering*) children an opportunity to study in a self-directed way.

    _____

4. Children (*learning*) valuable lessons at home.

    _____

5. The school environment often (*taught*) subjects in isolation from any practical application.

    _____

6. Many parents (*considering*) public education to be unsuccessful.

    _____

7. Parents (*appreciating*) the natural wonder and curiosity of children in home schooling.

    _____

8. Parents (*having*) the legal right to educate their children at home.

    _____

9. The education of children (*is*) a personal choice for parents.

    _____

10. Thousands of parents now (*agreeing*) with the idea of education at home.

    _____

8
verb

B. Look at a paper in progress, and identify the main verbs. Check to see that they are in a completed form. Remember, only simple present and simple past tenses can stand alone.

Summary Exercise

A. Interview the other students in your class, or talk to students from another class or from your dormitory. Write sentences about what you learn from them. You can ask questions about the students' country of origin, languages spoken, career goals, living arrangements on or off campus, and so forth. When you have finished writing this information, check carefully for correct present tense verb endings.

_____

_____

_____

_____

_____

_____

_____

_____

_____

_____

_____

B. Write a short biography about yourself in three paragraphs. Instead of using the first person *I,* use the third person *he* or *she.* Edit your work, carefully checking for correct third person *-s* endings.

C. Edit the following paragraphs. Pay special attention to the present tense verb endings.

A Typical Boy

Kit Fei Chan is a typical boy, just like many other boys who are born in Canton, China. His hometown is located in the countryside. Perhaps this place would not be preferable or attractive to city children because they would think it lack fun and modern conveniences. However, for the children in the country, it is almost like a paradise. They enjoy swimming, jogging, and playing group games. Kit Fei enjoy these games, too.

When Kit Fei and his family receives a visa to emigrate to the United States, he feel so sad because he know he is going to miss all his friends and relatives and the country roads he love to walk on. As soon as Kit Fei arrive in New York, he feel very strange about the new and different environment. He try very hard to adapt to his new life in America. He enter a bilingual school that provide him with many wonderful opportunities. He overcome his difficulties, make new friends, and graduate from high school.

Kit Fei get accepted to an American college, and he study very hard in order to achieve his goals. Through all his experiences he learn to meet the many challenges of life in a new country.

—Kit Fei Chan, College Student

8
verb

9

Irregular Verbs

English has many verbs that are irregular in the simple past and past participle forms. Through memorization and practice, these irregular verb forms will become familiar to you. Some of these verbs are included in the chart in this chapter.

Common Irregular Verbs

PRESENT	PAST	PAST PARTICIPLE
arise	arose	arisen
be	was/were	been
bear	bore	borne
begin	began	begun
bite	bit	bitten/bit
blow	blew	blown
break	broke	broken
bring	brought	brought
buy	bought	bought
catch	caught	caught
choose	chose	chosen
come	came	come
creep	crept	crept
dive	dived/dove	dived
do	did	done
draw	drew	drawn
dream	dreamed/dreamt	dreamt
drink	drank	drunk
drive	drove	driven
eat	ate	eaten
fall	fell	fallen
fight	fought	fought
fly	flew	flown
forget	forgot	forgotten
forgive	forgave	forgiven
freeze	froze	frozen

PRESENT	PAST	PAST PARTICIPLE
get	got	got/gotten
give	gave	given
go	went	gone
grow	grew	grown
hang	hung	hung
hide	hid	hidden
know	knew	known
lay	laid	laid
lead	led	led
lie	lay	lain
light	lit	lit
lose	lost	lost
prove	proved	proved/proven
ride	rode	ridden
ring	rang	rung
rise	rose	risen
run	ran	run
see	saw	seen
seek	sought	sought
set	set	set
shake	shook	shaken
sing	sang	sung
sink	sank	sunk
sit	sat	sat
speak	spoke	spoken
spring	sprang	sprung
steal	stole	stolen
sting	stung	stung
strike	struck	struck
swear	swore	sworn
swim	swam	swum
swing	swung	swung
take	took	taken
tear	tore	torn
throw	threw	thrown
wake	woke/waked	woken/waked/woke
wear	wore	worn
write	wrote	written

9
irreg

Exercise 1

A. In each sentence below, a correct or incorrect irregular verb form appears in parentheses. Edit each sentence to make the verb correct, or indicate that it's already correct. If necessary, consult the chart.

EXAMPLE   The snow (had ~~began~~ *begun*) to cover the Northeast.

1. The weather forecaster (*had chose*) to alert the television viewers to the impending snowstorm.

2. All the major networks (*had spoke*) of the storm for many days prior to its arrival.

3. Despite the television coverage of the storm watch, the snow (*had creeped*) into the area in the dead of night.

4. During the evening rush hour, commuters (*had drove*) without any problems, but in the morning, travel was impossible.

5. By early morning, people (*had woke*) up to find that the commute would be impossible.

6. Train service in and out of major cities (*had fallen*) behind schedule.

7. For one whole day, airplanes in area airports (*had not flew*).

8. Twenty-four hours after the storm (*had come*) to the area, people (*had forget*) that spring was coming soon.

B. Review the list of irregular verbs in the chart, and compose five sentences in which you correctly or incorrectly use the past or past participle form of an irregular verb. In a small group, exchange lists and edit your sentences. Discuss the changes you made or did not make.

_____

_____

_____

_____

_____

_____

9
irreg

_____

_____

_____

_____

 C. Look at a paper in progress, and underline any irregular verbs you see. Check for accuracy in form and spelling.

Verb Forms

Principle Parts of Verbs in English			
BASE FORM	**PAST**	**PRESENT PARTICIPLE**	**PAST PARTICIPLE**
REGULAR VERBS			
hope	hoped	hoping	hoped
live	lived	living	lived
want	wanted	wanting	wanted
IRREGULAR VERBS			
come	came	coming	come
eat	ate	eating	eaten
run	ran	running	run

10
verb

Most verbs are formed by combining one or more helping verbs with a main verb. The main verb plus any helping verb is called a **verb phrase.**

	verb phrase
ONE HELPING VERB	I **was walking** to school during the snowstorm.

	verb phrase
TWO HELPING VERBS	I **have been walking** to school for many years.

Helping verbs

Forms of Helping Verbs That Work Alone

BE
am, is, are
was, were
am being, is being, are being
was being, were being

MODALS
will, would
can, could
should
ought to
might, may
must
have to, has to, had to

HAVE
have, has
had

DO
do, does
did

Forms of Helping Verbs That Work Together

have	+ be	have been, has been, had been
all modals	**+ be**	will be
	+ have	will have
	+ have + be	will have been

Exercise 1

A. Read the following paragraphs, and underline the main verb(s) once and the helping verb(s) twice. The first sentence is marked for you.

My Last Year in High School

"I have never been so lost in my life before." These were my exact feelings when I graduated from high school. I was eighteen years old that year. I had become an adult, and my life had totally changed. I was going to be separated from my friends. I had to leave my high school where I had spent so many years. I had to say good-bye to my friends and teachers to whom I had become very attached. I cried a lot about this because I didn't want to grow up and face my unknown future by myself. I graduated from high school more in sorrow than in happiness.

My sweet memories of high school are the only things which I can have to carry on. As time passes, I realize that I don't have to stay with my friends all the time because my friends will remain in my heart.

—Wing Kwok, College Student

B. Look at another student's paper in progress, and underline the main verb(s) once and the helping verb(s) twice. Discuss the forms.

10
verb

97

Helping verbs and verb tense

In order to know which helping verb to use, you need to know which tense to use.

Verb Forms and Helping Verbs for Commonly Used Verb Tenses

The past, present, and future progressive use *be.*

PAST
subject + *was/were* + present participle
I **was** working in my studio yesterday.

PRESENT
subject + *am/is/are* + present participle
I **am** working in my studio right now.

FUTURE
subject + *will* (modal) + *be* + present participle
I **will be** working in my studio tomorrow.

The past, present, and future perfect use *have.*

PAST
subject + *had* + past participle
I **had** tried to call you all day.

PRESENT
subject + *have/has* + past participle
I **have** tried to call you all day.

FUTURE
subject + *will* (modal) + *have* + past participle
I **will have** called you by midnight.

10
verb

Exercise 2

A. Practice forming verbs in the past, present, and future progressive tenses. Choose the correct form of *be,* and write it in the space provided.

EXAMPLE   The international students on campus __*are*__ becoming very active. (present progressive)

1. We _____ forming an international students club last semester. [past progressive]

2. The president _____ planning many trips for international students this semester. [present progressive]

3. We _____ going to Washington, D.C., with the club next semester. [future progressive]

4. Students _____ visiting the United Nations in New York City in the fall of next year. [future progressive]

5. We _____ planning to go there last year, but we had no travel funds. [past progressive]

6. This semester we _____ budgeting our money more wisely. [present progressive]

B. Write a sentence about one thing that you *were planning to do* last semester, one thing that you *are planning to do* this semester, and one thing that you *will be doing* in a future semester. Use the correct verb form for the past, present, and future progressive tenses.

1. _____

_____

2. _____

_____

3. _____

_____

10
verb

C. Practice forming verbs in the past, present, and future perfect tenses. Choose the correct form of *have*, and write it in the space provided.

EXAMPLE   The international students _____ started forming a club. (present perfect)

1. The international students _____ begun to meet as a group over the summer before the semester started. (past perfect)

2. The club members _____ decided to meet every Thursday night this semester. [present perfect]

3. The students _____ written the agenda for the coming semester before the next meeting. [future perfect]

4. Last semester the students _____ hoped to accomplish many things. [past perfect]

5. This semester the club _____ decided to be more realistic about its goals. [present perfect]

6. The club's travel plans _____ decided by the end of the first meeting. [future perfect]

D. Write a sentence about one thing that you *had hoped to accomplish* last semester, one thing that you *have accomplished* this semester, and one thing that you *will have accomplished* by the end of this semester. Use the correct verb forms for the past, present, and the future perfect tenses.

1. _____

_____

2. _____

_____

3. _____

_____

Summary Exercise

A. Read the following sentences, and decide whether the verb form is correct or incorrect. If it is incorrect, make the necessary changes.

1. Ali will have finish the TOEFL test by noon today.

2. He has prepare very carefully for the exam.

3. While he is taking the test, his father will has a bite to eat in the cafeteria.

4. Ali feeling anxious about the exam late last night, but this morning he felt much better.

5. After he finishes the exam, he planning to look for an apartment in town.

6. The dormitories have be full since last week, so he must rent a place off campus.

7. First, of course, he will have try to find a newspaper.

8. His father will helped him to locate an apartment.

9. Together they can found an apartment within walking distance of campus.

10. After that Ali's college life can begin.

B. Working with a partner, read the following paragraph, and correct the faulty verb forms in the sentences by choosing helping verbs to complete the verbs. (If the verbs are either simple present or simple past, they do not need a helping verb.)

EXAMPLE   Many people~were~running in Central Park during the marathon.

The New York City marathon been a popular event for many years. Most of the runners training for many weeks before the event. The competitors be any age from their early twenties to their eighties. The course for the runners always been through the five boroughs of New York. Last weekend, the marathon racers began the race at noon in Central Park. It raining the night before, but the race started anyway. Traffic stopped in the park by barricades. The runners feeling nervous as the time to start came closer. Some of them not slept very well the night before. They worrying about the race and thinking of the many weeks of training that they had endure. The television camera crews aiming their cameras at the crowd. Each runner hoping to win because each had work very hard. The gun went off.

C. Look at a paper in progress to check your use of verb forms. Are you using the correct helping verbs? Are you using the correct present or past participles? Check your form and meaning.

11

Simple Present and Present Progressive

In English, both the simple present and the present progressive tenses can describe activities that happen in the present.

Present progressive

Use the present progressive tense to describe activities that are in progress.

subject + *am/is/are* + present participle
Rachael   **is   writing** a book.

In this sentence, it is clear that Rachael is in the process of writing a book. Many present progressive time expressions can be added to the sentence to show more precisely the time of the writing.

Some Common Present Progressive Time Expressions to Show Activities in Progress		
at the moment	this evening	this semester
right now	this month	this year
this afternoon	this morning	today

Rachael **is writing** a book **this semester.**
Now readers know that the activity is in progress over the semester.

Simple present

Use the simple present tense to describe activities that are factual or habitual. These activities occur in the present, but they are not necessarily activities in progress.

subject + verb (with *-s* if third person singular)

SHOWS FACT   The planets **revolve** around the sun.

SHOWS HABIT   The bus usually **arrives** late.

Some Common Time Expressions for Present Tense Habitual Activities		
all the time	every month	often
always	every semester	rarely
every class	every week	sometimes
every day	every year	usually
every holiday	most of the time	
every hour	never	

Choosing between simple present and present progressive

When you choose between the simple present and present progressive tenses, think about which time expression best describes the activity.

NOT APPROPRIATE All people are communicating in some language.
Is it happening only at the moment (present progressive)
or all the time (simple present)?

CORRECT All people communicate in some language.
This is a fact, and the correct tense must be simple present tense.

NOT APPROPRIATE The students are always speaking their own languages in class.
Do the students speak their own languages all the time as a habit (simple present), or is it happening at the moment or one time only (present progressive)?

CORRECT The students speak their own languages in class.
This is a habitual activity that occurs all the time, and the correct tense is simple present.

Verbs That Are Troublesome in Progressive Tenses		
	EXAMPLE	**OTHER USAGES AND MEANINGS**
SENSES		
see	I **see** the beauty.	Also: I **am seeing** that dentist. (meeting with, visiting, dating)
hear	I **hear** the birds.	Also: I **have been hearing** about the problem for a while. (receiving information)
smell	The flowers **smell** strong.	Also: I **am smelling** the flowers. (action in progress)
taste	The food **tastes** good.	Also: The cook **is tasting** the soup. (action in progress)
POSSESSION		
have	We **have** many friends.	Also: We **are having** a lot of fun. (experiencing)
own	They **own** many dogs.	
possess	She **possesses** much knowledge.	
belong	The book **belongs** to me.	

Verbs That Are Troublesome in Progressive Tenses

	EXAMPLE	OTHER USAGES AND MEANINGS
STATES OF MIND		
be	I **am** tired.	
know	I **know** the city well.	
believe	She **believes** in God.	
think	I **think** it is true. (know, believe)	Also: I **am thinking** about vacation. (having thoughts about)
recognize	His dog always **recognizes** him. (know)	
understand	The professor **understands** the equation.	
mean	I **don't mean** to pry. (don't want)	Also: I **have been meaning** to visit you. (planning, intending)
WISH OR ATTITUDE		
want	We **want** peace.	
desire	He **desires** his freedom.	
need	We **need** rain.	
love	Children **love** snow.	Also: I **have been loving** this book. (enjoying)
hate	Cats **hate** getting wet.	
like	He **likes** skiing.	
dislike	He **dislikes** skiing.	
seem	She **seems** gentle.	
appear	He **appears** tired. (seems to be)	Also: He **is appearing** at the theater. (acting, performing)
look	He **looks** tired. (seems to be)	Also: We **are looking** at photographs. (action of using eyes)

11
verb

Exercise 1

A. Choose either the simple present or the present progressive tense, and fill in the space provided in the sentence. Think about the reasons to use these two tenses. Remember that some words are never used in the progressive form.

EXAMPLE   John Wilson _____*has*_____ (*have*) three children.

1. He (*be*) _____ a single parent.

2. Every day he (*manage*) _____ a very busy schedule.

3. Right now he (*find*) _____ it helpful to talk to other people who (*cope*) _____ with the same difficulties as he is.

4. This semester he (*work*) _____ full time and (*take*) _____ one course at a local college.

5. Every week the children (*follow*) _____ a list of chores to help in the house.

6. The list (*hang*) _____ on the refrigerator.

7. John (*pay*) _____ the children a dollar for each job.

8. Every weekend he (*go*) _____ hiking or skiing in the nearby mountains with his children.

9. Now John (*know*) _____ how to juggle two jobs—housework and office work.

10. At the moment, John (*learn*) _____ to be a father, caretaker, and provider.

B. Write about the activities that you and your family members do monthly, weekly, and daily. What are the different responsibilities of each member of your family? Use frequency adverbs such as *always, sometimes, usually, often, rarely,* and *never.* Or, find out this information from a student in the class.

_____

_____

_____

_____

11
verb

_____

_____

_____

_____

_____

_____

_____

_____

_____

_____

C. Go to a public place, such as a library, a cafeteria, or a classroom. Observe the behavior of the people you see there, and write about their activities. Use the present progressive tense and some common time expressions.

_____

_____

_____

_____

_____

_____

_____

_____

_____

D. Write an ad for a roommate. Describe yourself and the activities that you do regularly and daily, so that the reader can get an idea about whether he or she would be compatible with you. Use the simple present tense and some common time expressions.

_____

_____

_____

_____

_____

11
verb

CHAPTER

12

Simple Past and Present Perfect

In English, both the simple past tense and the present perfect tense can describe activities that happened in the past.

Simple Past
subject + past tense verb

Present Perfect
subject + have/has + past participle

REASONS TO USE SIMPLE PAST	REASONS TO USE PRESENT PERFECT

1. An action occurred one time in the past.
    I **saw** that movie.
	1. An action occurred repeatedly in the past.
	    I **have seen** that movie two times.

2. An action occurred at a specific time in the past.
    I **met** your friend last week.
	2. An action that occurred at an unknown time in the past.
	    I **have** already **met** your friend.

3. An action was completed in the past and *does not* continue into the present.
    I **was** in the United States for one year. (I am no longer in the United States.)
	3. An action that occurred in the past and continues to the present.
	    I **have been** in the United States for one year. (I am still in the United States.)

Exercise 1

A. Read the following passage, and circle the correct verbs. To decide whether you need to use the simple past or the present perfect tense, ask yourself these questions.

Is the action something that happens once or is it repeated?
Does the action happen at a specific time or not?
Is the action still happening in the present?
Was it completed in the past?

Zoological Gardens

The first zoo (*was, has been*) founded in China in the twelfth century. Wen, the ancient Chinese king who (*started, has started*) it, (*wanted, has wanted*) to collect exotic animals from all over his empire. He (*kept, has kept*) them in a garden which he (*called, has called*) the Garden of Intelligence.

In ancient times many zoological collections also (*existed, have existed*) in Egypt and the Middle East. At that time wealthy people (*kept, have kept*) a great variety of wild animals for their personal collections.

During the eighteenth century, zoos (*were, have been*) built in Vienna and Madrid, and zoos (*became, have become*) open to the public. From that time to the present, people (*showed, have shown*) an interest in visiting zoos for entertainment. In addition, they (*learned, have learned*) many things about the animal world.

Although there are many notable zoos throughout the world, some of the largest zoos are in North America. They (*were, have been*) built in the Bronx; New York City; Washington, D.C.; and San Diego. Zoos (*entertained, have entertained*) people for many years. Going to the zoo (*became, has become*) not only a recreational activity but also an educational one for families.

Since the middle of the twentieth century, the increasing human population (*destroyed, has destroyed*) many animal habitats, thereby threatening the survival of certain animal species. Therefore, zoos (*became, have become*) places where endangered animal species can breed in protected areas.

B. Using the simple past or the present perfect tense, follow the directions below.

1. Write a sentence that describes a one-time action in the past. _____

   _____

   _____

2. Write a sentence that describes a repeated action in the past. _____

   _____

   _____

3. Write a sentence that descibes a past event with a specific time or date. _____

   _____

   _____

4. Write a sentence that describes a past event with no specific time or date. _____

   _____

   _____

5. Write a sentence that describes a past event that does not continue into the present.

   _____

   _____

6. Write a sentence that describes a past event that continues into the present.

   _____

   _____

C. Underline the simple past tense or the present perfect tense in the following sentences. With a partner, discuss the reason for using the simple past or the present perfect. Consider the following aspects of the action described in each sentence.

Is the action something that happens once, or is it repeated?
Does the action happen at a specific or nonspecific time?
Is the action still happening in the present?
Was the action completed in the past?

1. Kite flying has been a national pastime in some Asian countries for many centuries.

2. Chinese, Koreans, Japanese, and Malayans have used kites since approximately 1000 B.C.

3. In Asia people believed that kites would keep away evil spirits.

4. In China many people have enjoyed kite flying strictly for fun over the years, and they still do today.

5. In engineering, kites have been used to build bridges.

6. In meteorology, kites have carried weather recording instruments.

7. Kite-flying contests started long ago.

8. A kite-flying record has been achieved with a string of ten kites.

9. Kite flying has been popular along the seashore because of windy conditions.

10. In China the ninth day of the ninth month has been designated as Kite Day.

D. Choose one of the sentences in Exercise 1b and freewrite about that topic. Or write about traditional activities from your country that either are still practiced today or are no longer practiced.

_____

_____

_____

_____

_____

_____

_____

_____

_____

_____

_____

_____

_____

_____

Simple Past and Past Perfect

In English, both the simple past and past perfect tenses can describe activities that happened in the past. If there were *two actions* in the past and one occurred before the other, use the past perfect tense for the action that occurred first. Use the simple past tense for the action that occurred later.

EXAMPLE

           simple past   **past perfect**

By the time we **got** to the accident scene, the police **had arrived.** (The police arrived before we did.)

13
verb

Simple Past

Subject +past tense verb

Past Perfect

Subject + *had* + past participle

Exercise 1

A. Read the following paragraphs, and underline the verbs. Notice the use of the simple past and past perfect tenses.

The Forcing

I had been so happy. I had had a world that totally belonged to me: my country, my friends, my familiar places, even the sky. They had all been reality to me. I had had my dream. I had chosen my goals. All these had made up a glorious picture—my childhood during the time I was in China. However, just as each sentence has a period to symbolize the end, my life changed abruptly in the same way.

This picture of my life suddenly stopped with the sound of the airplane engines. The plane flew higher and higher; my heart said good-bye again and again. I had tried to say good-bye to everyone in that picture before I left, but the faces were still in my mind.

At that time, my parents were sitting next to me, but I still felt alone. I didn't want to say anything to them. They had changed my life. I knew they were bringing me to the United States so that my brother and I could have good educational and career opportunities. But, on the other hand, they had taken my happiness away and had pushed me into a dark hole, traveling in the airplane toward the unknown. It was as if I were blind. I was yelling, "Where is the sky?" All I could think to myself was, "What is more important—education or happiness?" Also, I asked myself, "Do I have any choices?" The answer was, "No, absolutely not." I could only choose the United States because I could not live alone at fourteen years of age. I realized that I had already dropped happiness in China and had accepted sadness in the United States by the time I landed in the new country.

"Good-bye China . . ."

—Ling Hoa Li, College Student

B. Write three sentences about things that you did before you came to the United States.

Before I came to the United States, I had already studied English for three years.

1. _____

_____

2. _____

_____

3. _____

_____

C. Review the following list of past events from the life of Ms. Betty Jackson. Write sentences from the information in the list, using the simple past and past perfect tenses. You may want to use the expressions *by the time*, *when*, *before*, and *after*.

1952: Born in New York City.
1955: Move to upstate New York with family.
1964: Graduate from elementary school.
1970: Graduate from high school.
1972: Take a year abroad in France.
1974: Move to Germany for six months.
1975: Graduate from college with a B.A. in French Language and Literature.
1979: Get married.
1980: First son is born.
1984: Receive a master's degree in English.
1985–1990: Teach English at a state university.
1987: Travel to Ireland.
1988: Teach in New York City.
1990: Travel to Japan to visit and work.
1994: Buy a house.
1995: Second son is born.

Ms. Jackson **had** already **traveled** to Ireland when she **went** to Japan.

Ms. Jackson **had not** yet **received** her master's degree in English by the time she **got** married.

1. _____

_____

2. _____

_____

13
verb

3. _____

_____

4. _____

_____

5. _____

_____

6. _____

_____

7. _____

_____

8. _____

_____

9. _____

_____

10. _____

_____

D. Develop a list of past events from a classmate's life, and write sentences about that person's life using the simple past and past perfect tenses.

_____

_____

_____

_____

_____

_____

_____

_____

E. Write a list of past events from your own life. Develop sentences using the simple past and past perfect tenses.

_____

_____

_____

_____

_____

_____

_____

_____

_____

_____

_____

_____

_____

13
verb

Simple Present and Future Perfect Tenses, and Future Time Clauses

In English, both the simple present and future perfect tenses can describe activities that will happen in the future. If *two actions* will occur in the future and one will occur before the other, use the future perfect tense for the action that will occur earlier. Use the simple present tense for the action that will occur later. Often, terms like *by the time, when,* and *before* are used to introduce the future time clause.

EXAMPLE   By the time we **graduate** from college, we **will have spent** many hours in the library. (We will spend many hours in the library before we graduate.)

| simple present   future perfect |

| **Simple Present** | **Future Perfect** |
| Subject + simple present | Subject + *have/has* + past participle |

Exercise 1

A. Think of things that you will have done by the time you graduate from college. Write three sentences.

EXAMPLE *By the time I graduate from college, I will have taken many English courses.*

1. _____

_____

2. _____

_____

3. _____

_____

14
verb

B. Think of things that you will have done by the time you return to your country. Write three sentences.

1. By the time I return to my country, _____

_____

2. _____

_____

3. _____

_____

C. Combine the following sentences, using the simple present tense in a future time clause and the future perfect tense in the main clause.

EXAMPLE I will receive my diploma from a college in the United States. I will return to my country. (*when*)

COMBINED When I **return** to my country, I **will have received** my diploma from a college in the United States.

1. My education will be finished. My life will change in many ways. (*when*) _____

_____

119

2. I will finish studying in the United States. I will learn a new way of life. (*by the time*)

_____

_____

3. I will receive my diploma. I will get married. (*before*) _____

_____

4. I will get a good job. I will have children. (*by the time*) _____

_____

5. I will work very hard in my profession. I will become successful. (*before*) _____

_____

D. Ask a classmate about his or her future plans. Find out what this person will have accomplished by the end of the week, by the end of the semester, by the end of the year, or in the next four years. Write down some of the answers in complete sentences.

_____

_____

_____

_____

_____

_____

_____

_____

_____

E. Freewrite about the ways in which you will have changed by the time you finish your college studies in the United States, discussing personality, family relationships, world knowledge, professional plans, and so on. Or freewrite about the ways in which your country will have changed by the end of the decade.

_____

_____

_____

_____

Conditionals

As a writer, you may at times want to express three types of ideas that are dependent on a condition or are imagined. These ideas may be (1) *true* in the present, true in the future, or possibly true in the future; (2) *untrue* or contrary to fact in the present; or (3) *untrue* or contrary to fact in the past.

Type I: Present true

Type I: True in the Present	
IF CLAUSE	**RESULT CLAUSE**
• Generally true as a habit or as a fact	
if + subject + present tense verb If I drive to school every day,	subject + present tense verb I get to class on time.
• True in the future as a one-time event	
if + subject + present tense verb If I drive to school today,	subject + future tense verb I will get to class on time.
• Possibly true in the future as a one-time event	
if + subject + present tense verb If I drive to school today,	subject + modal + base form verb I { may / might / could / should } get to class on time.

Exercise 1

A. Complete the following sentences by writing about things that you generally do as a rule or as a habit.

EXAMPLE   If I want to get exercise, *I work out at the gym.* _____

1. If I want to get exercise, _____
   _____.

2. If I want to relax, _____
   _____.

3. If I need to cook a special meal from my country, _____
   _____.

4. If I want to meet new friends, _____
   _____.

5. If I have extra money, _____
   _____.

B. Complete the following sentences by writing about things that are true in the future as one-time events.

EXAMPLE   If I write to my parents today, *they will receive the letter by Monday.* _____

1. If I write to my parents today, _____
   _____.

2. If we speak English every day, _____
   _____.

3. If I have a test tomorrow, _____
   _____.

4. If I study all night, _____
   _____.

5. If I work part time this semester, _____
   _____.

15
condit

123

C. Complete the following sentences by writing about things that are possibly true in the future as one-time events. Choose a modal to complete the result clause in each sentence.

EXAMPLE   If the snowstorm arrives tonight, *we may have a foot of snow by morning.*

1. If the snowstorm arrives tonight, _____
   _____.

2. If schools are closed tomorrow, _____
   _____.

3. If I want to be successful in my career, _____
   _____.

4. If we create a common world language, _____
   _____.

5. If we hope to have world peace,_____
   _____.

D. Finish this sentence: "If I win the lottery, I . . ." Working with a partner or in a group, pass your sentence to your neighbor so that he or she can write the next sentence. Continue this pattern to create a paragraph.

EXAMPLE   *If I win the lottery, I will travel around the world. If I travel around the world, I will have the chance to meet many interesting people. If I have the chance to meet many interesting people, . . .*

_____

_____

_____

_____

_____

_____

_____

_____

_____

_____

_____

_____

_____

_____

_____

Type II: Present untrue

Type II: Untrue in the Present	
IF CLAUSE	**RESULT CLAUSE**
if + subject + past tense verb	subject + { *would* + simple form of verb / *could* / *might* }
If I drove to school,	I { would / could / might } arrive on time.

15
condit

Writer's Alert

With the Type II conditional, when you use the verb *be* in the *if* clause, the form is always *were*.

I, you, he/she/it, we, they + *were*

NOT APPROPRIATE   If he **was** president, he would reform tax laws.

CORRECT   If he **were** president, he would reform tax laws.

Exercise 2

A. Complete the following sentences by writing about events that are untrue in the present.

EXAMPLE   If I won the lottery, _I would take a world cruise._

1. If I won the lottery, _____
_____.

2. If I were not a college student, _____
_____.

3. If I were a woman/man, _____
_____.

4. If I were president, _____
_____.

5. If the world were at peace, _____
_____

B. Finish this sentence: "If I were rich, I . . ." Working with a partner or in a group, pass your sentence to your neighbor so that he or she can write the next sentence. Continue this pattern to create a paragraph.

EXAMPLE   _If I were rich, I would give to charity. If I gave to charity, I would choose to help homeless people. If I chose to help homeless people, . . ._

_____
_____
_____
_____
_____
_____
_____
_____
_____

15
condit

_____

_____

_____

_____

_____

_____

Type III: Past untrue

Type III: Untrue in the Past	
IF CLAUSE	**RESULT CLAUSE**
if + subject + past perfect tense	subject + { *would* + *have* + past participle / *could* / *might* }
If I had driven to school,	I would not have been late.

Exercise 3

A. Complete the following sentences by writing about events that are untrue in the past.

EXAMPLE If I had not come to the United States, *I would never have had the opportunity to meet so many new people.*

1. If I had not come to the United States,_____

_____.

2. If I had not chosen to get a college degree, _____

_____.

3. If I had applied to a different college, _____

_____.

4. If I had studied French instead of English in my country,_____

_____.

5. If I had stayed in my own country, _____

_____.

B. Finish this sentence: "If I had decided not to go to college, I . . ." Working with a partner or in a group, pass your sentence to your neighbor so that he or she can write the next sentence. Continue this pattern to create a paragraph.

EXAMPLE *If I had decided not to go to college, I would have looked for a job in my country. If I had looked for a job in my country, . . .*

_____

_____

_____

_____

_____

_____

_____

_____

_____

Meaning and usage

Let's look at these examples to understand the meaning of conditionals.

Type I

CONDITION   If I **study** hard, I always **get** good grades.
This is true habitual behavior.

CONDITION   If I **study** hard for tomorrow's test, I **will get** a good grade.
This is true as a prediction of the future.

CONDITION   If I **study** hard for tomorrow's test, I **might get** a good grade.
This is possibly true as a prediction of the future.

Type II

SITUATION   I **don't have** enough money to go to Canada for vacation, so I **won't go.**
This is a true situation in the present.

CONDITION   If I **had** enough money to go to Canada for vacation, I **would definitely go.**
This is an imagined condition in the present.

Type III

SITUATION   I **did not have** enough money last month to go to Canada, so I **didn't go** there.
This is a true situation in the past.

CONDITION   If I **had had** enough money last month to go to Canada, I **would have gone** there.
This is an imagined condition in the past.

Expressing a continuous action with conditionals

If he **were living** in Hong Kong, he **would be spending** time with his family.
This is an untrue condition in the present because he is not living in Hong Kong.

If he **had been living** in Hong Kong last year, he **would have been spending** more time with his family.
This is an untrue condition in the past.

Writer's Alert

Sometimes you may want to express ideas about events that happen at different times, and you can shift from one tense to another to do this.

                          past
SITUATION   I **did not expect** to meet a lot of people from my country in the United
                          present
                 States, so I **am** surprised.

                          past
CONDITION   If I **had expected** to meet a lot of people from my country in the
                          present
                 United States, **I would not be surprised.**

129

Name: _____ Date: _____

Exercise 4

A. In each sentence of the following paragraph, decide which type of conditional you should use, and fill in the correct form. You may sometimes need to use different verb tenses and/or the passive form.

Life Without Electricity

We have much for which to thank Thomas Alva Edison, the great inventor of the nineteenth century, whose work with electricity changed the lives of all future generations. Life _____ (be) very different if it _____ (be, not) for the use of electricity. We _____ (live) a much simpler life in some ways if electricity _____ (invent, not) by Edison, and we _____ (have to) forgo many of life's conveniences. In fact, if suddenly we _____ (try) to live life without electricity, we _____ (find) that to do almost anything, we _____ (want) to use some form of electrical power. If it _____ (be, not) for electricity, we _____ (have, not) some of the greatest inventions of the twentieth century, such as motors, generators, telephones, radio and television, and computers. Our world _____ (be) a darker and duller place without electricity, and the pace of living _____ (be) a lot slower. What _____ life be like?

B. Read the following passage, and together with a partner underline the conditional forms. Discuss which type of conditional is used in each case.

Using a Common World Language

So many languages are spoken in the world. Different people speak different languages. The French speak French, the Chinese speak Chinese, and so on. If one common language were spoken in the world, it would serve as a bridge linking all countries together.

A common world language would help to keep world peace. The world is like a family, and the people who live in it should look upon each other as fathers, mothers, sisters, and brothers. As we know, if a family wants to live in harmony, it needs to have understanding among the family members. If a family wants to achieve understanding, its members must speak the same language. If the world family spoke a common language, there would be greater understanding among all people. If there were greater understanding, there would be fewer conflicts. If there were fewer conflicts, violence and wars would disappear.

In addition, if there were a common world language, difficulties for immigrants would be greatly reduced. I know this from my own experience. If I had been able to use a common language when I first came to the United States, my experience would have been much easier. I could have gone directly to college, and I might have worked successfully in an American company. For everyone, if we had a world language in common, what a wonderful life it would be! —Rafael François, College Student

 C. Choose one of the following Type I conditional sentences or write your own, and develop a paragraph about the topic.

If I have leisure time, I always enjoy being outside in nature.
If we develop a common world language, the world will be a better place.

_____

_____

_____

_____

_____

_____

_____

_____

_____

_____

_____

_____

 D. Choose one of the following Type II conditional sentences or write your own, and develop a paragraph about the topic.

If I could be any age, I would choose to be _____.
If I had my college degree, I would start my own business.

_____

_____

_____

_____

_____

_____

_____

_____

_____

_____

_____

E. Choose one of the following Type III conditional sentences or write your own, and develop a paragraph about the topic.

If the Europeans had not come to America, the fate of the Native Americans would have been very different.

If the automobile had not been invented, life in the twentieth century would be very different.

_____

_____

_____

_____

_____

_____

_____

_____

_____

_____

_____

_____

_____

CHAPTER

16

Active and Passive Voice

In English you can choose to use either active or passive voice for stylistic reasons (see 16d). All verbs in English may be written in the passive voice *except* the progressive forms of the present perfect, past perfect, future, and future perfect.

Verb Forms in the Passive Voice

TENSES	SUBJECT + *BE* FORM + PAST PARTICIPLE
PRESENT	The food **is prepared** by the chef.
PRESENT PROGRESSIVE	The food **is being prepared** by the chef.
PAST	The food **was prepared** by the chef.
PAST PROGRESSIVE	The food **was being prepared** by the chef.
PRESENT PERFECT	The food **has been prepared** by the chef.
PAST PERFECT	The food **had been prepared** by the chef.
FUTURE	The food **is going to be prepared** by the chef. The food **will be prepared** by the chef.
FUTURE PERFECT	The food **will have been prepared** by the chef.

16
voice

In all the sentences in the following chart, the agent of the action is not the subject, *food,* but rather *chef.*

Writer's Alert

Be sure to edit your passive verbs to check for correct forms. Each passive verb must have a form of *be* and a past participle. With regular verbs, the past participle will have the *-ed* ending. Sometimes it is difficult to hear these *-ed* endings in spoken English, so be careful to include them in your writing.

Name: _____ Date: _____

Exercise 1

A. Change the following verbs from active to passive voice.

1. write _____   10. discovered _____

2. wrote _____   11. had discovered _____

3. will write _____   12. will discover _____

4. has written _____   13. has discovered _____

5. is writing _____   14. is going to discover _____

6. had written _____   15. will have discovered _____

7. was writing _____   16. discover _____

8. is going to write _____ 17. was discovering _____

9. will have written _____ 18. is discovering _____

16
voice

B. Change the following verbs from passive to active voice.

1. was said _____   10. is told _____

2. has been said _____ 11. is being told _____

3. will be said _____   12. had been told _____

4. is going to be said _____ 13. was being told _____

5. had been said _____ 14. has been told _____

6. is said _____   15. was told _____

7. was being said _____ 16. will have been told _____

8. will have been said _____ 17. is going to be told _____

9. is being said _____ 18. will be told _____

C. Underline the verb in each sentence, and decide whether it is in the active or passive form. If the sentence is active, change it to passive. If it is passive, change it to active. If necessary, you may supply a *by* phrase to use as the subject of the active sentence. Make any other changes necessary.

EXAMPLE Sugar *is considered* an important food product. [passive]

People *consider* sugarcane an important food product. [active]

1. Sugar is produced in many countries. _____

_____

134

2. The sugarcane culture began in New Guinea. _____

_____

3. A warm, moist climate is required by sugarcane plants. _____

_____

4. At harvest the sugarcane is cut close to the ground by people using machetes or machines. _____

_____

5. Cultivators strip the leaves off the stalks, and trucks transport the sugarcane to a sugar mill. _____

_____

6. At the sugar mill, machines extract cane juice from the stalks. _____

_____

7. Most raw sugar is transported by ship to refineries to be washed and crystallized.

_____

8. The refineries produce the familiar white sugar. _____

_____

9. The sugar is packaged and sold in stores. _____

_____

10. Many people throughout the world consume sugar in large quantities. _____

_____

Use of the passive voice

In general, a writer can choose to use the passive voice for the following reasons. In each example below, the sentence written in the passive is more effective.

1. The agent of the action in the sentence is known, understood, or obvious.
   ACTIVE   The government **forced** drivers to drive at 55 mph.
   PASSIVE   Drivers **were forced** to drive at 55 mph.

2. The agent of the action is unknown.
   ACTIVE   Someone **stole** my passport.
   PASSIVE   My passport **was stolen.**

3. The agent of the action is unimportant.
   ACTIVE   People **told** me that Americans were friendly.
   PASSIVE   I **was told** that Americans were friendly.

4. You choose not to say who the agent of the action is.
   ACTIVE   The police officer **forced** him to confess.
   PASSIVE   He **was forced** to confess.

5. You simply want to vary your writing style and place emphasis on a different part of the sentence.
   ACTIVE   Many official dignitaries **visited** the Kremlin.
   PASSIVE   The Kremlin **was visited** by many official dignitaries.

6. You are using scientific or technical language.
   ACTIVE   The stem of the plant **transports** water and minerals.
   PASSIVE   Water and minerals **are transported** through the stem of the plant.

16
voice

Exercise 2

A. Think about the reasons for using the passive voice in English. Read the following sentences, and change them to the passive voice if it seems more effective. You can decide to keep the *by* phrase if it is needed for meaning. Then check with another student and discuss your reasons for using passive or active voice.

ACTIVE   Thieves **stole** the great masterpiece from the Chicago Museum.

PASSIVE   *The great masterpiece was stolen from the Chicago Museum. The agent is understood and obvious—reason 1.*

1. Last Thursday thieves stole a work of art from the Chicago Museum. _____

   _____

2. Picasso had painted the great masterpiece, which the museum displayed in the modern art section of the building. _____

   _____

3. The police believe that the robbers were wearing official museum uniforms. _____

   _____

   _____

4. The police are asking anyone who saw the thieves to contact the investigation bureau.

   _____

   _____

5. As soon as the police catch the thieves, the police will arrest them. _____

   _____

6. The thieves will sell the painting on the black market. _____

   _____

7. Sometimes criminals reproduce original paintings illegally. _____

   _____

8. They sell the reproductions as original paintings. _____

   _____

16
voice

9. The police must stop such acts of art fraud. _____

_____

10. The authorities have alerted international governments about this robbery. _____

_____

_____

B. Read the following paragraph, which uses technical and scientific language. Choose the correct tense and fill in the passive form of each verb in parentheses.

Radon

Radon is an inert gas. Radon _____ (*discover*) in 1900 by F. E. Dorn. This gas _____ (*call*) radium emanation. Since 1923 it _____ (*know*) as radon, and it _____ (*give*) the symbol Rn. Today, it _____ (*believe*) that nearly half of all the background radioactivity in the environment _____ (*make up*) of radon. Although radon _____ (*find*) in harmless quantities in many areas of the United States, some unsafe levels of radon _____ (*discover*) in homes throughout the country. This gas, which _____ (*call*) radon-222, _____ (*produce*) by the naturally occurring radium in the ground. Once it is present in the home, the gas _____ (*can, absorb*) into the lungs. It _____ (*estimate*) that annually 5,000 to 20,000 cases of lung cancer _____ (*cause*) by the presence of high quantities of radon in the home. The problem _____ (*can, alleviate*) through ventilation systems, but they can be costly.

C. Read the following paragraph about the martial arts, and together with a classmate underline each passive verb. Decide whether the passive voice is used appropriately. Decide why the author chooses to use passive voice.

The Martial Arts

The martial arts, which come from Japan, Korea, and China, were once used only for self-defense. As little as fifty years ago, these defensive arts were not even known in the United States. Today, however, we know that great skill and many years of rigorous training are required to master these sports. Judo, aikido, and jiujitsu come to the United States from Japan. In 1964 judo was accepted as an official Olympic sport. In this sport, the opponent must be pinned and held on the mat for thirty seconds in order for the other player to be declared a winner. Aikido is another defensive art in which players attempt to unite the mind and the body to accomplish victory. Jiujitsu is practiced by the Japanese military. The opponent is held in a position through the combined leverage, strength, balance, timing, and speed of the winner. In this way victory is achieved.

Tae kwon do, which comes from Korea, and kung fu, which comes from China, are also very popular defensive arts in the United States.

D. Write about a game, a sport, a cultural tradition, or a scientific phenomenon—for example, the game of chess, the rules of soccer, the Japanese tea ceremony, or the process of photosynthesis. Notice your use of passive or active voice.

_____

_____

_____

_____

_____

_____

_____

_____

_____

_____

_____

_____

_____

_____

_____

Verb Usage Review

A writer needs to consider different tenses and changes in voice when drafting a paragraph or essay. Look at the chapters in the "Using Verbs" section of this book to help you with any verb usage problems you may be having.

Exercise 1

Underline the verbs in the following passages. Identify which tense the writer is using, and discuss the reasons with a partner.

A.

Something Old, Something New

When I first came to the United States, I felt very happy and excited. After a few weeks, I experienced culture shock. It happened when I saw a couple kissing in the street in public. I had never seen that before in my country. I had to learn the new life-style so slowly . . . and gradually I began to adapt to the new culture. I was afraid of losing my native culture because I felt it would be a great waste if I lost what I had already learned in China.

What I want for my new life is to adapt to a new culture and also to retain my own Chinese way of life. I often read Chinese books to retain some of my country's ways while I am trying to assimilate into the new culture of the United States. I am doing this by going to school and making new friends. Compared to others I have assimilated very slowly, but I am proud of myself because I haven't forgotten my own culture. I believe that in the future I will have melted into the new culture completely while keeping my own.

—Raymond Ren, College Student

B.

A Fable from my Culture

Once there were three men with only one bottle of wine. All three of them wanted to have the wine, but there was just enough wine for one person to drink. An old man came and suggested to them that each one should draw a picture of a snake.

He said, "The one who is the fastest will get the wine."

They all agreed that this was the best way to decide who was going to drink the wine, so they started to draw. One of the three finished so fast that the other two had not even started yet.

He thought, "I have so much time that I will draw four legs on my snake to make it more beautiful." Then he announced, "I am finished."

But the old man handed the wine to the man who had finished second. "Snakes do not have legs; something with legs is not a snake anymore," he explained.

Moral: If you do more than what you are asked to do, you will surely spoil the result.
—Li Ting Chen, College Student

C.

My Future Husband

A good marriage is very important in our lives. Because you will live with your mate for the rest of your life, it is essential to choose someone who suits you. My husband-to-be will have the following qualities: he will have a stable job, he will share in the housework, and he will have a sense of humor.

First of all, my future husband will have a stable job with a future. Many marriages end in divorce because of money problems in the family. However, if my husband and I both can work, we will be able to save for the future: we will buy a new house and a new car, and we will travel to other countries.

Second, my husband must be responsible in sharing in the housework with me. Each of us will return to our house tired after work, and neither of us will be superior to the other, so both of us should do the housework. Whoever gets home first must be willing to do the work at home. If we do this, we will argue less and our marriage will be more stable.

Third, my husband will have a good sense of humor. Sometimes if a marriage is stable, life can become a little boring. If my husband is humorous, he will make my life more surprising and fun. His humor will take away the stress of daily life. If I do something he doesn't like, he will tell me in a funny way to let me realize my mistakes. Our family will not be a serious family, but rather it will be a funny family.

I believe that if my husband has these three characteristics, our marriage will be a very happy one that we will enjoy very much.
—Laihung Leung, College Student

D.

The Year 2000

I hope the year 2000 is coming very soon. By the year 2000 in China, there will be many wonderful changes in our country. By that time, China will have become the "four modernizations" country. By this time people will no longer need to worry about getting products. Everyone will have been able to get food. Peasants will no longer work in terrible weather. Everyone will work inside and control machines with computers. The "computer world" will have arrived in China. There will be no disease, no starvation, no struggle, and no pollution. Everyone will be equal, and everyone will go to school and receive a good education. This is my vision of China in the year 2000.

—Hai Yan Gao, College Student

17
verb

CREATING AGREEMENT AND USING MODIFIERS

Subject-Verb Agreement

To be verbs and helping verbs

Watch out for the following troublesome verbs that change form according to person or tense. Be sure to select the correct verb form so that your subject and verb agree.

- *Be* verbs (present and past)

I **am/was**
You (sing., pl.)
We   } **are/were**
They

He
She   } **is/was**
It

- Helping verb *be* in the present progressive and past progressive tenses

Present progressive

I **am** talking.
You
We   } **are** talking.
They
He, She, It **is** talking.

Past progressive

I
He, She, It } **was** talking.
We
You   } **were** talking.
They

To *have* verbs and helping verbs

- *Have* verbs (present)

I
You
We
They
} **have** a new home.

He, She, It **has** a new home.

- Helping verb *have* in the present perfect and present perfect progressive tenses

Present perfect

I
You
We
They
} **have** been here for many years.

He, She, It **has** been here for many years.

Present perfect progressive

I
You
We
They
} **have** been living here for a long time.

He, She, It **has** been living here for a long time.

18
s-v agr

Name: _____ Date: _____

Exercise 1

A. Choose the correct form of *be* or *have*.

EXAMPLE   Wei ___*is*___ studying abroad.

1. I _____ a foreign student.

2. I _____ been living in the United States for one year.

3. Right now my family _____ living in the city near my college.

4. We _____ happy to be together.

5. Some of my friends _____ not as fortunate as I _____.

6. Some students _____ families in countries far away.

7. They _____, therefore, occasionally homesick.

8. Aya _____ a student from Japan.

9. She _____ a large family in Osaka.

10. She _____ learning to be very independent in the United States this semester.

11. Hoiling _____ a student from China.

12. She _____ not been back to her home country in two years.

13. Roksolana _____ family members in Boston, and she _____ some relatives still in Ukraine.

14. They _____ together as often as possible.

15. We _____ many classmates whose families are either in the United States or in their home countries.

B. Write three sentences about your life abroad, or write three sentences about your parents' lives. Use *be* and *have* as main verbs or helping verbs.

_____

_____

_____

18
s-v agr

_____
_____
_____
_____
_____

C. Look at your partner's sentences and rewrite them, substituting the pronouns *we, you,* and *they* for *I.*

_____
_____
_____
_____
_____
_____

Do or *does*

- *Do* or *does* to show emphasis

  | I, You, We, They | **do** enjoy hiking! |
  | He, She, It | **does** enjoy hiking! |

- *Doesn't* or *Don't* to show the negative

  | I, You, We, They | **don't** exercise enough. |
  | He, She, It | **doesn't** exercise enough. |

- Present tense for all other verbs in the third person singular. You must add *-s* to the verb.

  | I, You, We, They | **walk** every day. |
  | He, She, It | **walks** every day. |

Writer's Alert

In English there are many nouns, called **mass** or **noncount nouns,** which use the singular form. Look out for these nouns as the subjects of your sentences, and make sure the verbs are singular.

Name: _____ Date: _____

Exercise 2

A. Rewrite the following sentences in two ways.

Use both *do* and *does* to show strong emphasis.
Use *don't* and *doesn't* to show the negative.

EXAMPLE Teenage drivers need supervision.

Teenage drivers do need supervision.

Teenage drivers don't need supervision

1. Many parents understand the behavior of teenagers.

_____

_____

2. To be effective, parents need to remember their own youth.

_____

_____

3. A teenage child requires extra understanding and patience.

_____

_____

4. Some adolescents respect the opinions of the older generation.

_____

_____

5. Certain young adults sympathize with the concerns of parents.

_____

_____

B. Write three sentences like those in Exercise 2a, and ask a partner to change the sentences by showing emphasis or the negative.

_____

_____

_____

_____

_____

_____

_____

C. Choose one of the sentences from Exercise 2b to serve as a topic sentence, and develop a paragraph to support your ideas. Use *do* and *does* to show emphasis and use *don't,* and *doesn't* to show the negative in your writing.

_____

_____

_____

_____

_____

_____

_____

_____

_____

_____

Name: _____ Date: _____

Summary Exercise

A. Read the following paragraph. Write *S* above each subject and *V* above each verb. Then edit the sentences for subject-verb agreement. The first sentence is done for you.

Islam

       S   *V* *is*
Islam ~~are~~ a religion that was officially founded in A.D. 622. Islam is related to

Judaism and Christianity. It have many followers, second in numbers only to those

of the Christian faith. Mohammed, the great prophet and leader of Islam, were born

in 570 in Mecca in western Arabia. His followers is called Muslims, and they have

many important codes of behavior that must be followed. There is four pillars of Islam:

fasting for the holy month of Ramadan; praying five times a day; giving *zakat,* which

are donations to the needy; and making a pilgrimage once in a lifetime to Mecca.

Muslims obeys the rules of Islam, and they tries to follow a moral life. The rules of

Islam is written in the holy book called the Koran. Muslim people believes in the

integrity of all religions. Today we still does have the opportunity to visit many beau-

tiful mosques built many years ago, and we are reminded of the beginnings of Islam.

—Farhan Naqvi, College Student

B. Read the following paragraph. Write *S* above each subject and *V* above each verb. Then edit the sentences for subject-verb agreement. The first sentence is done for you.

The Importance of Friendship

      S   *V*
Friend is the most important word in my life. This word mean a lot to me. I love

to make friends, and since I am an active person, I am often the one who initiate a

conversation with others. I can't stand loneliness; thus, finding someone to share tears

and laughter are very important to me.

    In America it has been a painful experience for me to be separated from my friends.

Since I have been here, letters, cards, and packages from my friends has given me a

lot of encouragement. Checking the mailbox are the most exciting moment every

day.

Making new friends are a good way to help me adapt myself to a new environment. I have friends from different countries which includes England, Japan, Thailand,
and Korea. Through my friends I can learn about new cultures. All of my friends is the
precious gifts in my life.   —Wing Kwok, College Student

 C. Write *S* and *V* above all the subjects and verbs of a classmate's writing. Check for
subject-verb agreement and discuss your choices.

 D. Write *S* and *V* above all the subjects and verbs of the sentences you have written in a
paragraph or essay. Check for agreement of subject and verbs.

18
s-v agr

Agreement with Quantifiers

Expressions followed by a plural noun and a singular verb

Each of
Each one of
Every one of } **plural noun + singular verb**
One of   the ESL **students lives** on campus.
None of

Expressions followed by a plural noun and a plural verb

Several of } **plural noun + plural verb**
Many of   the **students live** off campus.
Both of

Expressions followed by either a singular or a plural verb

In the following cases, the noun after the expression determines the verb form. If the noun is noncount or collective, it takes a singular verb. If the noun is plural, it takes a plural verb.

Some of
Most of } **noncount noun + singular verb**
All of   the **produce is** fresh.
A lot of

Some of
Most of } **plural noun + plural verb**
All of   the **vegetables are** fresh.
A lot of

Much and *most* with noncount and plural nouns

Look at the following examples, and be sure to watch for these errors in your writing.

quantifier + noncount noun

NOT APPROPRIATE   Much ~~of~~ traffic occurs during rush hour.

CORRECT   **Much traffic** occurs during rush hour.

quantifier + plural noun

NOT APPROPRIATE   Most ~~of~~ Americans live in the cities or suburbs.

CORRECT   **Most Americans** live in the cities or suburbs.

Name: _____ Date: _____

Exercise 1

A. Complete the following sentences by choosing either a singular or plural verb.

EXAMPLE **Each of** the oldest boys in many traditional families _____has_____ (have) many responsibilities.

1. Most of the eldest sons in many families (*be*) _____ chosen to be the care-takers for the parents and the managers of the families' financial affairs.

2. Every one of them (*be*) _____ considered the family's future hope.

3. Both of the parents in the family (*teach*) _____ the eldest son how to conduct family matters.

4. Many of the younger children (*possess*) _____ less experience and knowledge than the eldest.

5. Each of the younger children (*be*) _____ required to follow the advice and the guidance of the eldest son.

6. All of the eldest children in a family (*serve*) _____ as role models for the younger children.

7. Both of the parents (*bequeath*) _____ the majority of their wealth to the eldest child.

8. Some of the disadvantages of being the firstborn (*be*) _____ the responsibility, the pressure, and the hard work.

9. Three of the advantages (*be*) _____ the respect, the authority, and the satisfaction.

10. Each of these disadvantages and advantages (*be*) _____ experienced by the firstborn child.

B. Read the following text. Make the verbs singular, by adding -s, or plural, by adding nothing.

Gender Bias in America's Classrooms

Many of the recent studies on gender bias confirm _____ that discrimination against female students still occur _____ frequently in American classrooms. Some of the elementary and secondary classroom teachers across the nation believe _____ this is impossible. Nonetheless, every one of the studies reveal _____ that many of our teachers give _____ more attention to male students than to female students. In addition, it has been found that much of the curriculum ignore _____ or stereotype _____ females. A lot of the gender bias in classrooms undermine _____ girls' confidence and dissuade _____ them from taking math and science courses. As a result, none of our female students hope _____ to escape the discrimination that subtly discourage _____ them from participating in education as freely as their male counterparts. Studies have, in fact, revealed that most of the boys in America's elementary and secondary classrooms speak _____ out eight times more often than the girls.

C. Working with a partner, look at the following paragraph and edit for subject-verb agreement.

Traditional China

China is a traditional country where many of the ideas about boys and girls is based on age-old customs. According to tradition, many of the girls in the family has to do a lot of the housework, and most of them is not allowed to pursue a higher education. A lot of parents feels that their daughters won't rebel against parents' wishes if they are without education. A long time ago in Shanghai, many of the girls has bandaged feet so that they couldn't go outside. By contrast, the boys have better positions than girls. All of the boys doesn't do any housework, and most of them is encouraged to get a good education. Chinese parents still support the education of their sons even if one of the sons' ability are not very high. Parents always think the boys are more capable than the girls. Those different positions are unfair for girls.

Yuen Ling Yu, College Student

19
s-v agr

155

D. Write about the roles or positions that girls and boys experience in your country. How are the expectations different for each? Use expressions of quantity as much as possible to explain the different life and job experiences of men and women in your country.

_____

_____

_____

_____

_____

_____

_____

_____

_____

_____

_____

_____

_____

_____

_____

E. Exchange papers with another student, and check for subject-verb agreement. Suggest ways in which the writer might use quantifiers to improve the draft.

CHAPTER

20

Paired Conjunctions

Paired conjunctions like *both . . . and, either . . . or, neither . . . nor,* and *not only . . . but also* pose some problems for subject-verb agreement.

Both . . . and always needs a plural verb, whether the elements being joined by the conjunction are singular or plural.

both . . .   **and**   **+**   **plural verb**
Both the president **and** her advisor **are** in Tokyo this week.

both . . .   **and**   **+**   **plural verb**
Both the president **and** her advisors **are** in Tokyo this week.

Either . . . or, neither . . . nor, and *not only . . . but also* may take either a singular or a plural verb. The subject closer to the verb determines the form of the verb.

singular subject   **+ singular verb**
Either the president or her **advisor**
Neither the president nor her **advisor**   **is** in Tokyo.
Not only the president but also her **advisor**

plural subject   **+ plural verb**
Either the president or her **advisors**
Neither the president nor her **advisors**   **are** in Tokyo.
Not only the president but also her **advisors**

Exercise 1

A. Combine the following sentences, using the paired conjunctions in parentheses. Think about subject-verb agreement.

EXAMPLE   The president is responsible for keeping campaign promises. The vice president is responsible for keeping campaign promises. (*not only . . . but also*)

COMBINED   *Not only the president but also the vice president is responsible for keeping campaign promises.*

1. The president has given speeches about reinventing and improving government. The vice president has given speeches about reinventing and improving government. (*not only . . . but also*) _____

    _____

2. The president does not want to make false promises to the electorate. The vice president does not want to make false promises to the electorate. (*neither . . . nor*)

    _____

    _____

3. Channel 4 televises the campaign speeches and debates. Channel 2 televises the campaign speeches and debates. (*either . . . or*) _____

    _____

4. Important political advisors are always present at these events. Important members of both political parties are often present. (*not only . . . but also*) _____

    _____

5. Newspaper reporters are eager to attend political debates. Television reporters are eager to attend political debates. (*not only . . . but also*) _____

    _____

6. Writers in national newspapers analyze and discuss the details of the political speeches and debates. Guests on television talk shows analyze and discuss the details of the presidential speeches and debates. (*not only . . . but also*) _____

    _____

7. The news media keep the people informed about political issues and promises. The print media keep the people informed about political issues and promises. (*both . . . and*)

_____

_____

8. In many speeches the president has promised to reform the health-care system. The vice president has promised to reform the health-care system. (*both . . . and*)

_____

_____

9. The younger voters do not want to continue paying high taxes without benefits. The older voters do not want to continue paying high taxes without benefits. (*neither . . . nor*) _____

_____

B. Combine the following sentences, using the paired conjunctions of your choice. Consider the relationship of the ideas in the two sentences, and think about subject-verb agreement.

1. The United States has four seasons. Hong Kong has four seasons. _____

_____

2. Japanese cars are economical. Korean cars are economical. _____

_____

3. Italian cooking is often spicy. Spanish cooking is often spicy. _____

_____

4. The Chinese do not drink coffee. The Japanese do not drink coffee. _____

_____

5. Coffee is available in American restaurants. Tea is available in American restaurants.

_____

C. Interview a classmate about his or her country, and compare what you learn about such things as climate, cuisine, products, customs, language, and sports to what you know about your own country. Write sentences using paired conjunctions to combine two noun subjects. Think about subject-verb agreement, and have your partner check your work.

EXAMPLE   Not only the Chinese language but also the Korean language has a complicated writing system.

_____

_____

_____

_____

_____

_____

_____

_____

_____

_____

_____

_____

_____

D. Compare and contrast school life in your country with school life in the United States. Use paired conjunctions to express your ideas more clearly.

_____

_____

_____

_____

_____

_____

_____

_____

_____

_____

_____

_____

_____

21

Separated Subjects and Verbs

When phrases or clauses come between the subject and the verb of the sentence, you need to check for agreement carefully.

PHRASES

NOT APPROPRIATE A person <u>with sensitive eyes</u> have to wear sunglasses.

CORRECT A **person** <u>with sensitive eyes</u> **has** to wear sunglasses.

CLAUSES

NOT APPROPRIATE A person <u>whose eyes are sensitive</u> have to wear sunglasses.

CORRECT A **person** <u>whose eyes are sensitive</u> **has** to wear sunglasses.

21
s-v agr

Writer's Alert

When the subject is the same in both the main clause and the dependent clause, the verbs must agree.

NOT APPROPRIATE A person <u>who want to protect her eyes</u> wears sunglasses.

same subject

CORRECT A **person** <u>who **wants** to protect her eyes</u> **wears** sunglasses.

Exercise 1

A. Fill in the blank in each sentence with a verb that agrees with the subject.

EXAMPLE   People from all over the world _____*enjoy*_____ sports.

1. The people of Brazil _____ the game of soccer.

2. Many young people who live in China _____ the game of Ping-Pong, or table tennis.

3. The game of baseball _____ both in America and in Japan.

4. A popular sport in England, France, Australia, New Zealand, and South Africa _____ rugby.

5. Ice skating, which originated in the Scandinavian countries, _____ popular wherever the winters are cold enough.

B. Read the following paragraph, and edit for subject-verb agreement. Write *S* over the subjects and *V* over the verbs. Underline the phrase or clause that separates the subject from the verb.

EXAMPLE   The facts <u>about children and bicycle safety</u> ~~is~~ startling.
                        S   *V are*

Bicycle Safety

Many bicycle accidents involving children occurs on quiet residential streets. However, these accidents, which cause thousands of visits to the emergency room annually, is preventable. Therefore, bicycle safety education for children are vital to the well-being of all young people. The causes of most bicycle accidents are riding into main roads without stopping and turning onto other roads without yielding. Furthermore, children, who are more vulnerable to injury than adults, has undeveloped peripheral vision, poor judgment of speed, and a distinct lack of a sense of danger. While it is a fact that an impact to the head can lead to serious injury, many parents do not insist that their children wear helmets. Parents who understand the facts about bicycles and safety makes their children wear helmets. Helmets on children riding bicycles save lives!

C. Copy a paragraph from one of your papers or a book, but replace the verbs with blanks (as in Exercise 1a). Exchange paragraphs with a partner, and fill in the blanks your partner's paragraph. Work together to check your answers.

Other, Others and Another
as Pronouns and Adjectives

Pronouns

When *others*, *the others*, and *the other* are used as pronouns in a sentence, they require particular grammatical patterns.

Pronouns

OTHERS + PLURAL VERB
Adds points about a topic; there may be more points.

> I enjoy Paris for many reasons. Some reasons are the beautiful architecture and gardens; **others are** the wonderful people, culture, and language.

THE OTHERS (PLURAL) + PLURAL VERB; *THE OTHER* (SINGULAR) + SINGULAR VERB
Adds the last point or points about the topic; there are no more.

> There are fourteen people on the tour. Half the people want to visit museums; **the others want** to go hiking.

> I have two travel books. One is about New Zealand, and **the other is** about Australia.

Exercise 1

A. Read the following short paragraphs, and decide whether to use the pronouns *others,* *the others,* or *the other* to complete the sentences.

EXAMPLE   There are several reasons to visit Europe. One reason is to meet new people.

_____*Others*_____ are to experience new foods and customs.

1. In Korea, it is vital to pursue a college degree for two reasons. One is a cultural rea-

    son. _____ is an economic reason.

2. Speaking different languages can be very useful. Some benefits are travel and social

    opportunities. _____ are professional and educational opportunities.

3. Being an avid reader can serve a person in three important ways. One way is to open

    up the world of knowledge. _____ are to open up the world of creativ-

    ity and imagination.

B. Complete the following short paragraphs by deciding whether to use the pronouns *others, the others,* or *the other* to complete the sentences. Exchange papers with a partner, and correct each other's work.

EXAMPLE   New York City has many interesting places to visit. One is *the Empire State*
Building . *Others* are *the World Trade Center and Rockefeller Center*.

1. There are many wonderful places to visit in my country. Some are_____.

    _____ are _____.

2. A good teacher should have three important qualities. One is _____.

    _____ are _____.

3. I have two favorite foods. One is _____.

    _____ is _____.

C. Develop short paragraphs below in the same manner as in Exercises 1a and 1b by using *others, the others* or *the other* as pronouns in two sentences following the first sentence. Choose one of the short paragraphs for the beginning of a freewriting.

My future husband/wife must have three characteristics.
I have two favorite sports.
Living in the twenty-first century will bring many changes.

22
agr

165

_____
_____
_____
_____
_____
_____
_____
_____
_____
_____
_____
_____
_____
_____

Adjectives

Another, other, and *the other* are sometimes used as adjectives in a sentence, and they require particular grammatical patterns.

Adjectives

***ANOTHER* + SINGULAR NOUN**
Adds an idea about the topic; there may be more ideas.

***OTHER* + PLURAL NOUN**
Adds more ideas about the topic; there may be more ideas.

> There are some reasons to visit California. One reason is to see the beautiful landscape. **Another reason** is to meet interesting people.

> **Other reasons** to visit California are the weather, the ocean, and the mountains.

***THE OTHER* + SINGULAR OR PLURAL NOUN**
Adds the final point or points to be discussed.

> There are two very important sights to see in Paris. One is the Louvre Museum, and **the other one** is the Cathedral of Notre Dame.

> There are many sights to see in Paris. One sight is the Louvre Museum. **The other sights** are the Eiffel Tower, the Champs-Élysées, the Cathedral of Notre Dame, and the Arc de Triomphe.

Name: _____ Date: _____

Exercise 2

A. Read the following short paragraphs, and decide whether to use the adjectives *another*, *other*, or *the other* to complete the sentences.

EXAMPLE   There are some reasons I like living off campus. One reason is the privacy.

_____*Another*_____ reason is the independence.

1. When I lived in the dormitory, there were two problems. One problem was the lack of privacy. _____ problem was the noise at night.

2. If you want to meet new people, you must do several things. One good idea is to frequent public places like restaurants, libraries, and movie theaters. _____ ideas are to join sports clubs and to volunteer your time in organizations.

3. In order to maintain your automobile, you should do two things. One thing is to always check the oil level. _____ is to get tune-ups.

B. Complete the following short paragraphs by deciding whether to use the adjectives *another*, *other*, or *the other*. Exchange papers with a partner and correct each other's work.

EXAMPLE   Americans are very interested in keeping fit for many reasons. One reason is

_____*for health*_____

_____*Another*_____ reason is *for beauty* _____.

1. The fitness craze is popular for many reasons. Some reasons are _____.
   _____ reasons are _____.

2. Traveling can be great for two reasons. One reason is _____.
   _____ reason is _____.

3. In order to be a successful language learner, it is important to do certain things. One thing is_____.
   _____ thing is _____.

22
agr

167

C. Develop short paragraphs below in the same manner as in Exercises 2a and 2b by using *another*, *other*, or *the other* as adjectives in two sentences following the first sentence. Choose one of the short paragraphs for the beginning of a freewriting.

Common steps to follow to have your dream date
The features of your favorite city
Reasons you love the spring

Summary Exercise

Read the following passage, and underline all the forms of *others, the others,* or *the other* as pronouns or *another, other,* and *the other* as adjectives. Discuss with a partner which form is used.

Reasons I Miss the Spring in Japan

There are many reasons why I miss the springtime in Japan. When the spring flowers such as tulips and daffodils start to bloom in the northeast of the United States, I remember two wonderful aspects of spring in Japan. One is the small pink petals of the cherry blossoms, and the other is the sweet smell of the blooms. The cherry blossom is the national flower of Japan, and it seems to me that the Japanese love the cherry blossoms best among all flowers.

During the spring in Japan, many people celebrate in many ways. One way is to pack a picnic lunch and go to the park. Another way they enjoy celebrating is to sing to karaoke and dance. There are stands along the sidewalks which sell food and collectibles to the passersby. Some sell sweets and hot noodles. Others sell old-fashioned toys and spring plants.

Regardless of age or gender, everybody enjoys the short period of cherry trees in full bloom. At night the blossoms are lit up by lights placed between the trees. In the dim light some people find the world very romantic; others think it is mysterious. The ponds quietly reflect the cherry blossoms and the lamplight. Although I feel sad that the pink petals fall so soon, one senses the beauty of transience, which the Japanese feel is worth it. Sentimentality is the reason for the popularity of cherry blossoms in Japan.

—Kiyomi Sekiya, College Student

22
agr

Demonstrative Adjectives

Besides subjects and verbs, other elements in a sentence must agree. **Demonstrative adjectives** or **pronouns** (*this, that, these,* and *those*) must be either singular or plural, depending on the noun being modified.

MIXED   This crystals of water make snowflakes.

BOTH PLURAL   **These crystals** of water make snowflakes.

MIXED   Those snowflake crystal is made of frozen water.

BOTH SINGULAR   **That snowflake crystal** is made of frozen water.

23
agr

Name: _____ Date: _____

Exercise 1

A. Read the following sentences, and fill in the correct word. Choose *this, these, that,* or *those.*

EXAMPLE   Americans are busily engaged in all forms of exercise. _____*This*_____

exercise can be in many different forms.

1. Many Americans are going on diets to improve their health. Magazines often popularize

    _____ diets through advertising.

2. Beautiful models are seen on the covers of many magazines in America.

    _____ models are always in perfect condition.

3. Looking good is becoming a fad in America. _____ fad is reaching peo-

    ple of all ages, particularly _____ people over forty.

4. People gain confidence through improving their appearance. _____ con-

    fidence is important to their sense of well-being and can help them in all aspects of their

    lives.

5. Fitness clubs have become extremely popular over the years. _____ pop-

    ularity is due to the desire of most people to stay in shape as they grow older.

B. Write pairs of sentences like those in Exercise 1a. Write the first sentence, and have
a partner write the second sentence, using *this, these, that,* or *those* to modify the noun in
the second sentence. Exchange sentences, and correct each other's work.

EXAMPLE   *Information about preventative medicine is helpful.*

PARTNER   *This information is available in certain magazines.*

1. _____

    _____

    Partner: _____

    _____

    _____

2. _____

   _____

   Partner: _____

   _____

3. _____

   _____

   Partner: _____

   _____

 C. Look at a paper in progress, and notice your use of demonstrative adjectives. Check closely for agreement with singular or plural nouns.

Adjectives in a Series

When you use two or more adjectives in a series, you need to place them in the correct order before the main noun. The following chart explains the categories and the order of adjectives in English.

DETERMINER	QUALITY	PHYSICAL DESCRIPTION		NATIONALITY	MATERIAL	QUALIFYING NOUN	MAIN NOUN
that	expensive	smooth	black	German	fiberglass	racing	car
our	friendly	big	old	English		toy	spaniel
four	little	round	white		plastic	Ping-Pong	balls
several	beautiful	young	red	Japanese		maple	trees

Exercise 1

A. Read the following sentences, and underline all the adjectives. Decide which category each adjective belongs to.

EXAMPLE Bird-watchers have the *satisfying*, *solitary* pleasure of witnessing the activities of *seasonal* birds.

1. We have seen many wonderful ground-feeding birds outside our house at our bird feeder.

2. There are usually several big black birds that come to our bird feeder during the cold winter months.

3. The kind of bird food and the type of bird feeder you choose will determine the different varieties of birds that will come to the feeder.

4. Small feeders will attract small, delicate birds; large, heavy birds will feed at big feeders.

5. All the birds enjoy the shelter of our many beautiful tall oak shade trees.

B. Write sentences to describe a special person, place, or possession. Use at least two adjectives to describe the main noun. Check the chart for the correct order of adjectives.

1. _____

   _____

2. _____

   _____

3. _____

   _____

C. Exchange sentences with a partner, and add adjectives to each sentence. Use at least two adjectives to describe the main noun. Check the chart for the correct order of adjectives.

1. _____

_____

2. _____

_____

3. _____

_____

D. Look at a paper in progress, and find the nouns in your sentences. Decide whether you can improve the writing by adding adjectives to describe the nouns.

24
agr

USING GRAMMATICAL STRUCTURES

Fragments

A **sentence fragment** is part of a sentence treated as a complete sentence, with a capital letter at the beginning and a period at the end. A fragment may lack an important sentence element such as a subject or a verb, thus confusing readers by leaving out crucial information.

SUBJECT MISSING   Began pumping water out of the basement.
   READER'S RESPONSE: Who was pumping, or what was doing the pumping?

EDITED   **The fire truck** began pumping water out of the basement.

VERB MISSING   The insurance company responsible for the costs.
   READER'S RESPONSE: What did the company do?

EDITED   The insurance company **became** responsible for the costs.

Fragments may be phrases or clauses mistakenly asked to stand on their own as sentences. Such fragments make readers do the writer's job, forcing them mentally to reattach a word group to a nearby sentence.

FRAGMENT   They were able to get the pump started again. **By replacing the gas filter.**
   The second statement is a modifying phrase detached from the preceding sentence.

EDITED   They were able to get the pump started again **by replacing the gas filter.**

Recognizing sentence fragments

Sentence fragments occur in all shapes and sizes. Some are easy to identify, others less so. To edit effectively, however, you need to be able to identify word groups lacking a subject or a verb and to recognize clauses detached from sentences to which they belong.

1 Look for a subject and a verb

A **complete sentence** must contain both a subject and a complete verb, expressed or implied. If a word group punctuated as a sentence lacks either, it is a fragment.

FRAGMENT   Yet also needs to establish a family counseling program.
> **READER'S RESPONSE:** This doesn't say *who* (or *what*) needs to establish the program. The fragment is lacking a subject.

EDITED   Yet the **Community Health Clinic** also needs to establish a family counseling program.

FRAGMENT   The new policy to determine scholarship size on the basis of grades rather than on the basis of need.
> **READER'S RESPONSE:** This doesn't indicate anything about what the new policy *does* or *is*. The fragment is lacking a complete verb.

EDITED   The new policy **determines** scholarships on the basis of grades rather than on the basis of need.

Writer's Alert

In checking for fragments, be careful not to mistake a verbal for a verb. A **verbal** is part of a verb acting as a noun or modifier. Verbals include participles (*testing, tested*), infinitives (*to test*), and gerunds (*testing*). A verbal alone can never act as the verb in a sentence. When combined with a helping verb (such as *is, has, can,* or *should*), a verbal can be part of a complete verb (*was testing, should test*).

FRAGMENT   The laboratory **testing** the samples for traces of platinum.

COMPLETE SENTENCE   The laboratory **was testing** the samples for traces of platinum.

Exercise 1

Read the following sentences, and decide whether each is a complete sentence or a fragment. Look for subjects and complete verbs. If the sentence is incomplete, correct it by adding either a subject or a complete verb.

EXAMPLE   ___*fragment*___ Computer science ^*is* becoming a popular field.

1. _____ Many college students interested in computer science.

2. _____ Computer science changing the fields of communication, trans-

    portation, and medicine.

3. _____ Began revolutionizing society a few decades ago.

4. _____ By improving the field of communication.

5. _____ Direct and immediate communication now possible.

6. _____ Fax machines responsible for better business.

7. _____ Transportation possibilities have been greatly advanced.

8. _____ Air transportation, automobiles, and trains have benefited from

    computer technology.

9. _____ Medical technology improving because of the development of

    highly specialized equipment.

10. _____ Computer scientists working diligently to improve our lives.

Look for subordinating words and sentence fragments

A word group containing both a subject and a complete verb may still be a sentence frag-ment if it is controlled by a subordinating word (such as *although, because, that,* or *since*) that turns it into a modifier. Placed at the beginning of a clause, subordinators tell readers to regard the word group as part of a larger statement, as a subordinate (dependent) clause needing to be attached to a main clause that it qualifies or modifies.

MAIN CLAUSE
Potential homebuyers have learned about the low crime rate and the excellent school system.

MODIFYING CLAUSE
Because potential homebuyers have learned about the low crime rate and the excellent school system.
This clause cannot act as a complete sentence.

25
frag

Because potential homebuyers have learned about the low crime rate and the excellent school system, demand for housing in the area has risen considerably in the past few years.

Strategy

To identify subordinate clause fragments, look for a word group beginning with a subordinating conjunction such as *after, although, if, because, unless,* or *since* or with a relative pronoun (*that, what, which,* or *who*). Then check whether this word group is attached to a main clause. If it is not, then it is a fragment.

25
frag

Exercise 2

Read the following sentence pairs, and decide whether they are complete sentences or sentence fragments. Correct all the sentence fragments. Supply any information necessary to make complete sentences, or attach a fragment to an adjacent main clause.

EXAMPLE   Even though the majority of Americans ate dinner out at least once last week,
M
p̸ost prefer home-cooked meals.

1. In retailing, "impulse" purchases are small, inexpensive items. That are found near the cash registers and checkout lanes of stores.

2. According to a consumer analyst. Eating dinner out is an impulse purchase for most Americans.

3. For over 50 percent of Americans. The decision to eat out is made on the spur of the moment.

4. Although they would prefer to eat home cooking, many people end up eating out. Because it saves time.

5. Even if restaurants were easily affordable. A large number of people would prefer eating at home.

6. While many people eat out because it is easier. Others eat out to socialize with friends.

7. Young adults eat in fast-food restaurants more often than older Americans. Despite the fact that older, more affluent Americans eat in expensive restaurants most often.

8. Because Americans give in to their food impulses. Most restaurant meals are bought on impulse.

Strategies for editing sentence fragments

You can correct sentence fragments in four different ways. As you edit, choose the Strategy that best suits the particular kind of fragment, your purpose for writing, the meaning you wish to emphasize, and the stylistic effect you wish to create.

Strategy 1

Supply the missing sentence element.

FRAGMENT (LACKS VERB)
Several arguments favor allowing adopted children to contact their natural parents. **Among the most important the need to find out about any hereditary diseases.**

EDITED
Several arguments favor allowing adopted children to contact their natural parents. Among the most important **is** the need to find out about any hereditary diseases.

Strategy 2

Attach the fragment to a nearby main clause. Rewrite the passage if necessary.

FRAGMENT (SUBORDINATE CLAUSE)
Modern trauma centers are equipped to give prompt care to heart attack victims. **Because rapid treatment can minimize damage to heart muscles.**

EDITED
Modern trauma centers are equipped to give prompt care to heart attack victims because rapid treatment can minimize damage to heart muscles.

Strategy 3

Drop a subordinating word so the subordinate clause can act as a complete sentence (main clause).

FRAGMENT
Although several people argued strenuously against the motion. It passed by a considerable majority nonetheless.

EDITED
Several people argued strenuously against the motion. It passed by a considerable majority nonetheless.

Strategy 4

Rewrite a passage to eliminate the fragment.

FRAGMENT
Some sports attract large numbers of participants in their fifties, sixties, and even seventies. **For example, tennis and bowling.**

REWRITTEN
Some sports, **such as tennis and bowling,** attract large numbers of participants in their fifties, sixties, and even seventies.

Exercise 3

A. Choose two different editing strategies, and correct each of the sentence fragments in the following pairs.

EXAMPLE Studies have proved that friendships are vital. For the sake of your health.

Studies have proved that friendships are vital for the sake of your health.

Studies have proved that friendships are vital. They are vital for the sake of your health.

1. Because friendships have been shown to be crucial to our health and well-being. People are encouraged to seek the support and affection of friends to ease the daily stress of our lives.

_____

_____

_____

_____

2. In fact, people who have friends are less likely to suffer from disease. Knowing they can turn to others for advice and affection.

_____

_____

_____

_____

3. Furthermore, those who are afflicted with disease are quicker to recover. When they have friendship and support.

_____

_____

_____

_____

25
frag

4. For example, in a study of heart patients. Those patients who lacked a spouse or confidant recovered more slowly than those who had a strong support group.

_____

_____

_____

_____

5. Support groups may be as powerful as medicine. One of the most important influences on healing being among loving friends.

_____

_____

_____

_____

6. Yet in the busy and very mobile lives of most Americans. Making and maintaining friendships can sometimes be difficult.

_____

_____

_____

_____

7. Friendships are still a vital part of living a happy and healthy life. Although it can be a challenge to keep long-distance relationships.

_____

_____

_____

_____

B. Working with a group, look through newspapers, magazines, or textbooks, and identify ten sentence fragments. List them, and indicate which fragments are missing either a subject or a verb or both and which are fragments containing a subject and a verb introduced by a subordinating word. Discuss strategies to edit the fragments.

C. Write a paragraph about the importance of friendship in your life. Then, edit your writing for fragments, and correct them using the strategies listed in this chapter.

_____

_____

CHAPTER

27

Parallelism

Parallelism is the expression of similar or related ideas in similar grammatical form, as in the following sentence.

> I furnished my first
> apartment with **purchases | from department stores,**
> **items | from the want ads,**
> and **gifts | from my relatives.**

Parallelism enables you to present ideas concisely while highlighting their relationships.

Parallelism can also offer pleasure and surprise. You can use it to create intriguing sentence rhythms while highlighting unexpected images and contrasts. Once you begin a parallel pattern, however, you need to complete it. Incomplete or **faulty parallelism** (with mixed structures) disappoints readers' expectations and may make sentences confusing and hard to read.

Readers generally find a sentence with parallel elements easy to read and understand. They also appreciate the touch of style parallelism can bring even to everyday sentences.

MIXED   Consider swimming if you are looking for exercise that **aids** cardiovascular fitness, **develops** overall muscle strength, and **probably will not cause** injuries.

PARALLEL   Consider swimming if you are looking for exercise that **aids** cardiovascular fitness, **develops** overall muscle strength, and **causes** few injuries.

In deciding which parts of a sentence to make parallel and how to write them, you should consider the meaning as well as the emphasis you wish to create. In order to employ effective parallel structure in your writing, you need to consider these three sentence elements: words, phrases, and clauses.

Words, phrases, or clauses in a series

Whether you create parallelism with words, phrases, or clauses, you need to make sure all the elements employ the same grammatical forms. When you place items in a series, make sure they are parallel in grammatical form. Using mixed grammatical categories can make a series clumsy and distracting.

WORDS — MIXED To get along with their parents, teenagers need to be patient, tactful, and **to display tolerance.**

WORDS — PARALLEL To get along with their parents, teenagers need to be patient, tactful, and **tolerant.**

PHRASES — MIXED The singer Jim Morrison is remembered for his innovative style, his flamboyant performances, and for behavior that was self-destructive.

PHRASES — PARALLEL The singer Jim Morrison is remembered for his innovative style, his flamboyant performances, and **his self-destructive behavior.**

CLAUSES — MIXED In assembling the research team, we looked for engineers whose work was innovative, with broad interests, and who had boundless energy.

CLAUSES — PARALLEL In assembling the research team, we looked for engineers whose work was innovative, **whose interests were broad, and whose energy was boundless.**

Writer's Tip

In creating parallelism, make sure you repeat all words necessary to the meaning of a sentence, including all the words called for by grammatical structures or idiomatic expressions. You need not repeat a lead-in word, however, if it is the same for all elements in a series.

Mosquitoes can breed in puddles, ~~in~~ ponds, and ~~in~~ swimming pools.

If the lead-in words differ, you must include them.

You need to **chop** the cilantro, **grind** the coconut, and **grate** the nutmeg.

As you edit, read each series with the structure of the full sentence in mind so you can decide what words are necessary to the meaning.

Name: _____ Date: _____

Exercise 1

A. Read the following sentences, and underline the parallel elements. Circle the coordinating conjunctions that signal the parallel elements. Write on the line whether it is *words, phrases,* or *clauses* that make the sentence in good form.

EXAMPLE   Visiting a new country (and) learning a new language can be wonderful!

                                                            phrases

1. I came to the United States, I saw many new and unusual sights, and I conquered the new life-style. _____

2. I hoped to meet many people and to learn many things in the United States.

    _____

3. At first the climate and the cuisine seemed very different. _____

4. Then, I had to adjust to the new language, accomodate to the new culture, and integrate the new customs. _____

5. Soon I realized that living in a new country and embracing a new culture were essential to learning a new language. _____

6. I decided that I should get to know people who were familiar with the new culture and who were fluent in the new language. _____

7. How to meet people and where to meet people were my two problems.

    _____

8. I consciously went to the library, the cafeteria, and the gym as often as possible.

    _____

9. In no time I had met a lot of interesting people, and I had begun to feel at home in my new country. _____

10. Live and learn—I had found that life was exciting, challenging, and worthwhile.

    _____

27
II

B. Revise the following sentences by making the sentence elements parallel. Think about *words, phrases,* and *clauses.*

MIXED   Early humans began to use tools, utensils, and they sat by the fire to make life easier.

PARALLEL   <u>Early humans began to use tools, utensils, and fire to make life easier.</u>

1. It is important to note that life changed dramatically for early humans when they learned to use fire and caves were important.

    _____

    _____

2. It is believed that the cold prompted them to take embers from a natural fire and bringing it to a cave.

    _____

    _____

3. They used fire to chase the animals in a hunt, to protect themselves when they rested, and they used fire to harden their spears. _____

    _____

    _____

4. But the wonder of fire was more than warmth, more than protection, and it was more than practical help in making weapons. _____

    _____

    _____

5. The wonder of fire was that it lengthened the daylight hours, it allowed people to work at night, and to sit by the fire and talk. _____

    _____

    _____

6. The fire also gave early humans a sense of home where there was comfort, security, and the children waited there. _____

    _____

    _____

27
II

7. The keeper of the fire was probably a member of the clan who was older and he or she was also wiser. _____

_____

_____

8. The old ones had survived difficulties, avoided accidents, and they used their intelligence to reach old age. _____

_____

_____

9. The cave gave the early people a place to make tools, they stored food there, and a place to cure animal hides. _____

_____

_____

10. Later on, these cave dwellers began to paint on the walls and using their fires for ceremonies. _____

_____

_____

C. Write three sentences of your own using *words*, *phrases*, and *clauses* in parallel form. Exchange papers with a partner, and decide which sentence elements are used.

1. _____

_____

2. _____

_____

3. _____

_____

Paired elements joined with coordinating conjunctions

Use parallel grammatical structures when you connect sentence elements with a coordinating conjunction (*and, but, or, for, nor, so,* or *yet*). The parallelism will direct your readers' attention to the relationship of the elements and make the sentence easier to read.

LACKS PARALLELISM

A well-trained scientist learns to keep a detailed lab notebook and make the entries accurately.

PARALLEL WORDS

A well-trained scientist learns to keep a **detailed and accurate** lab notebook.

LACKS PARALLELISM

First-year chemistry courses are supposed to teach students how to take notes on an experiment and the ways of writing a lab report.

PARALLEL PHRASES

First-year chemistry courses are supposed to teach students **how to take notes on an experiment** and **how to write a lab report.**

LACKS PARALLELISM

Because she is interested in science and organizing complex information intrigues her, Lynn has decided to become a technical writer.

PARALLEL CLAUSES

Because she is interested in science and she is intrigued by organizing complex information, Lynn has decided to become a technical writer.

27
//

Exercise 2

Combine the following pairs of sentences by joining sentence elements—words, phrases, and clauses—with coordinating conjunctions (*and, but, or, nor, for, yet,* or *so*).

SEPARATE   The Caribbean Sea has beautiful flora.
                 The Caribbean Sea has beautiful fauna.

COMBINED   *The Caribbean Sea has beautiful flora and fauna.*

1. The Caribbean Basin is isolated from other world waters.
   The Caribbean Basin has different wildlife.

   _____

   _____

2. This body of water is bordered by Central and South America.
   It is bordered by the Atlantic Ocean.

   _____

   _____

3. The barrier of land prevents migration of tropical marine species.
   The barrier of cold water prevents migration of tropical marine species.

   _____

   _____

4. Because of the isolation of the waters, the marine species of the Caribbean Basin are unique.
   Because of the evolution of separate wildlife, the marine species of the Caribbean Basin are unique.

   _____

   _____

5. The spectacular flora and fauna are appreciated by professional divers.
   The spectacular flora and fauna are appreciated by amateur divers.

   _____

   _____

6. Environmentalists hope to preserve the area's natural beauty.
   The Caribbean Basin has become increasingly popular.

   _____

   _____

7. Awareness of the fragile quality of marine life should help prevent destruction of the area.
   Realization of the need to preserve this wildlife should help prevent destruction of the area.

   _____

   _____

8. Divers who enjoy the beautiful Caribbean Basin must respect this delicate balance.
   Divers who appreciate the beautiful Caribbean Basin must respect this delicate balance.

   _____

   _____

Paired elements joined with correlative conjunctions

When you wish to call special attention to a relationship or a contrast, you may wish to use pairs of connectors such as *both . . . and, not only . . . but also, either . . . or, neither . . . nor,* and *whether . . . or* (known as correlative conjunctions). You need to use parallel form for the elements you are joining.

Our dilemma is clear: **either** we must reduce manufacturing costs **or** we must file for bankruptcy.

Correlative conjunctions are also effective strategies for organizing sentences with long phrases or clauses.

ORIGINAL
People in this country claim to marry "for love," yet their pairings follow clear social patterns. They choose partners from the same social class and economic level. Most marriages bring together people with similar educational and cultural backgrounds. Similarities in race and ethnic background are important as well.

EDITED (CORRELATIVE CONJUNCTIONS ADDED)
People in this country claim to marry "for love," yet their pairings follow clear social patterns. They choose partners **not only with the same class and economic background but also with the same educational, cultural, racial, and ethnic background.**

The items you link with a correlative conjunction should be clearly related in meaning and similar in grammatical form.

Exercise 3

Create sentences about information in the chart by joining sentence elements—words, phrases, and clauses—with correlative conjunctions (*both . . . and, not only . . . but also, either . . . or, neither . . . nor*).

COUNTRY	LOCATION	POPULATION (MILLIONS)	PRINCIPAL LANGUAGES
China	Asia	1,000	Mandarin, Cantonese
France	Europe	55	French
Haiti	Caribbean	5	French, Creole
United States	North America	230	English
Italy	Europe	60	Italian
Great Britain	Europe	57	English
Australia	Pacific	17	English
Argentina	South America	32	Spanish
Vietnam	Asia	62	Vietnamese, French
Madagascar	Africa	12	Malagasy, French
India	Asia	853	Hindi, English
Japan	Asia	124	Japanese

EXAMPLE   *People speak English not only in the United States but also in Great Britain, Australia, and India.*

1. _____
   _____

2. _____
   _____

3. _____
   _____

4. _____
   _____

5. _____
   _____

6. _____
   _____

7. _____
   _____

8. _____
   _____

9. _____
   _____

10. _____
    _____

Summary Exercise

A. Read the following student sentences, which employ effective parallel structure. Underline the parallel elements, and circle any coordinating conjunctions or correlative conjunctions.

EXAMPLE   People who are not Japanese think <u>that we always work hard,</u> <u>that we never show affection to one another,</u> (and) <u>that we are always polite.</u>

1. I miss my beautiful, powerful, and successful country, China.

2. Japan has maintained not only high technology but also a beautiful culture and strong spirit.

3. The landscape makes you half tipsy, the people make you feel warm, and the word *China* leads you into a Xanadu.

4. I love Taiwan because it is the place where I was born and the place where I live.

5. Russia, my ardently loved motherland, has not only a long history but also many wonders with fascinating scenery.

6. Mexico's economy is growing, its technology is advancing, and its education is improving.

7. There are a lot of beautiful places, interesting stories, and delicious foods in Thailand.

8. The birds are singing, the flowers are giving off fragrant smells, and the trees are growing—all are the nature of my country, Korea.

9. My country, Pakistan, has beautiful cities, exciting hillsides, and soothing beaches.

10. Japan has four seasons, which are green spring, blue summer, yellow fall, and white winter.

11. My country is very famous for great sight-seeing in Dae-Gu, the beautiful ocean in Pusan, and delicious food in Cheon-An.

12. Ukraine is beautiful in its traditions, rich in its natural resources, and friendly in its people.

205

13. The Kunlun mountain range is her body; the Great Wall is her backbone; the Yellow River is her blood; the capital, Beijing, is her heart. She is just my own country—China.

14. Coming to my country, Vietnam, tourists can enjoy beautiful weather, taste different tropical fruits, and visit many clean white beaches all year round.

 B. Write some sentences to describe your country, using the ideas of parallel structure in this chapter.

_____

_____

_____

_____

_____

_____

_____

_____

_____

_____

_____

_____

_____

_____

C. Show the sentences from Summary Exercise b to a classmate, and ask him or her to identify parallel elements.

 D. Look at a thesis statement in a draft you are working on. Notice whether your sentence is well balanced and in good parallel form. Revise it, using the ideas from this chapter about parallel structure.

Coordination and Subordination

This chart shows the different structures you can choose when using coordination or subordination.

COORDINATION		SUBORDINATION		
COORDINATORS	**CONJUNCTIVE ADVERBS**	**NOUN CLAUSES**	**ADJECTIVE CLAUSES**	**ADVERB CLAUSES**

, and
, but
 	
, or
, nor
, for
, yet
, so
	; in addition,
	; in contrast,
	
	; otherwise,
	
	; however,
	; therefore,
		that clauses
		
		yes/no question clauses
		
		wh- question clauses
			who
			whom
			which
			that
			whose
			when
			why
				Time
				  until
				  when
				  after
				  since
				
				Reason
				  because
				  since
				  as
				
				Condition
				  if
				  unless
				
				Contrast
				  although
				  even though
				  though
				  while
				  whereas

It is good composition style to use the four varying sentence types in your writing: the simple sentence, the compound sentence, the complex sentence, and the compound-complex sentence.

Using coordination to form a compound sentence

When you combine two simple sentences to make a compound sentence, you can use a coordinating conjunction, a conjunctive adverb, or a semicolon.

Coordinators		
COORDINATING CONJUNCTION	CONJUNCTIVE ADVERB	MEANING
, and	; in addition, ; furthermore,	add an idea
, but	; in contrast,	opposite idea
, yet	; however, ; nonetheless,	
, so	; therefore, ; thus, ; consequently,	result
, for		because
, or	; otherwise,	choice
, nor		also not

These are just some of the conjunctive adverbs you can choose in your writing.

COMPOUND SENTENCE

             main clause   +   **main clause**
The helicopter is a versatile aircraft, **and** it can be used for many kinds of jobs.

COMPOUND SENTENCE

             main clause   +   **main clause**
The helicopter is a versatile aircraft; **therefore,** it can be used for many kinds of jobs.

COMPOUND SENTENCE

             main clause   +   **main clause**
The helicopter is a versatile aircraft; it can be used for many kinds of jobs.

Exercise 1

A. Form compound sentences by combining the following pairs of sentences. Choose any of the three methods of coordination: comma plus coordinating conjunction, semicolon plus conjunctive adverb plus comma, or semicolon.

EXAMPLE   The United States is made up of forty-eight contiguous states. It also includes Alaska and Hawaii.

The United States is made up of forty-eight contiguous states, but it also includes Alaska and Hawaii.

1. Nevada is a popular western state where gambling is legal. Many people come to gamble and to see the celebrities who perform in this state.

   _____

   _____

   _____

2. Utah has many wonderful national parks, canyons, and deserts. Utah has the famous Salt Lake, which is four times as salty as any ocean.

   _____

   _____

   _____

3. Washington's largest city, Seattle, is one of America's most popular cities. It is a growing state.

   _____

   _____

   _____

4. Tennessee is famous for the birth of America's music. Elvis Presley, the famous king of rock and roll, lived in Tennessee.

   _____

   _____

   _____

28
clause

5. New Orleans, located in Louisiana, is one of America's busiest ports. Jazz was first played in this state.

_____

_____

_____

B. Read the following paragraph, and combine sentences by using any of the three methods of coordination used in Exercise 1a.

I often think about my home country. I want to know the news whenever possible. When I read in the newspapers, the first word I want to read is *China*. I like to read articles about the relationship between China and the United States. I hope their relationship becomes better and better. Some articles make me happy. Some articles make me angry. Many articles that discuss aspects of China do not seem accurate to me. Most Americans believe what they read because they know only a little about China. Therefore, I often tell my friends about Chinese society. I tell them about how China is changing to a better and better place. I also try to predict the future of China. I try to discuss my opinions with my American friends. I discuss these facts with my Chinese friends. China is my home country, and I will keep watching it.

—Xiang Ke Chen, College Student

Using subordination to form a complex sentence

When you combine a simple sentence with a dependent clause to form a complex sentence, you use a subordinating conjunction.

Subordinating Conjunctions		
after	once	whether
although	provided that	which
as soon as	rather than	while
because	so/so that	who/whoever
before	though	whom/whomever
even though	until	whose
how/however	when/whenever	
if	where/wherever	

	subordinate clause	main clause

| COMPLEX SENTENCE | **After** the invention of the helicopter in the 1930s, this aircraft became very useful in rescue missions. |

	main clause	subordinate clause

| COMPLEX SENTENCE | Many rescue missions have been successful **because** helicopters take off and land vertically. |

Writer's Alert

It is necessary to use coordinators or subordinators when you write different sentence types, but you must be careful not to mix the two grammatical structures.

MIXED **Although** frogs can live both on land and in water, **but** they need to breathe oxygen.

This sentence has both a subordinator, *although,* and a coordinator, *but.* You must use one pattern, but not both.

main clause

CORRECT COORDINATION Frogs can live both on land and in water, **but** they need to
main clause
breathe oxygen.

subordinate clause

CORRECT SUBORDINATION **Although** frogs can live both on land and in water, they need to
main clause
breathe oxygen.

28
clause

Exercise 2

A. Form complex sentences by combining the following pairs of sentences using subordination.

EXAMPLE Hawaii became part of the United States. There were forty-nine states.

Before Hawaii became part of the United States, there were forty-nine states.

1. Pennsylvania is famous for chocolate. The world's largest chocolate and cocoa factory is in Hershey, Pennsylvania.

   _____

   _____

2. North Carolina is famous for flying. The first successful air flight in the world took place in this state.

   _____

   _____

3. The world's first atomic bomb was set off in New Mexico in 1945. This bomb was built in that state.

   _____

   _____

4. The world's first professional baseball game was played in Hoboken, New Jersey. Few people realize this event happened in New Jersey.

   _____

   _____

5. Kentucky is most often thought of as Abraham Lincoln's birthplace. Kentucky has the world's largest Braille publishing house.

   _____

   _____

B. Revise the following paragraph, using subordination to combine sentences and form complex sentences.

I came to the United States. I found that people of different races sometimes live separately. White people have white friends. Black people have black friends. Asian people have Asian friends. Most people are always in their own cultural group. It is more comfortable than being with different ethnic groups. Most of us stay in our own groups. We have many misunderstandings, prejudices, and stereotypes about one another. The differences in cultural background lead to the separation between people. We can try to get along with and accept people of all races, cultures, and backgrounds. We cannot change our own way of being. 　　　　　　　　　—Yuko Makitani, College Student

Using coordination and subordination to form a compound-complex sentence

When you combine two main clauses and a dependent clause, you use both coordination and subordination.

COMPOUND-COMPLEX SENTENCE

subordinate clause
Because the helicopter can fly in any direction and hover in midair, it can

main clause　　　　　　　　　　　　　　　**main clause**
maneuver in many places, **and** it can be useful for all kinds of jobs.

28
clause

Name: _____ Date: _____

Exercise 3

Combine the following groups of sentences by using coordination and subordination to form compound-complex sentences. Each sentence will have both a coordinator and a subordinator. Circle the coordinators and subordinators. Remember punctuation.

EXAMPLE

Florida is a peninsula.

It has the second-longest coastline in the United States.

Florida's waters have a great abundance and variety of fish.

(Because) Florida is a peninsula, it has the second-longest coastline in the United States, (and) its waters have a great abundance and variety of fish.

1. Millions of tourists come to California each year.
   They visit Hollywood, Disneyland, and Death Valley.
   They visit the giant sequoia trees.
   These trees are the largest living things in the world.

   _____

   _____

   _____

2. Texas is the second-largest state in the United States.
   This state is famous for cowboys and rodeos.
   Many famous cowboys lived and died in Texas.

   _____

   _____

   _____

3. Ohio was the birthplace of eight U.S. presidents.
   Other famous people came from Ohio.
   Thomas A. Edison, the Wright brothers, and John D. Rockefeller, Sr., were all born in this state.

   _____

   _____

   _____

4. Michigan is known for manufacturing more trucks and cars than any other state.
   Michigan also has eleven thousand lakes.
   The longest suspension bridge connects two parts of the state.

   _____

   _____

   _____

5. New York State has the biggest city in the country.
   New York has huge national parklands as well.
   Outdoor sports enthusiasts visit these parklands every year in all seasons.

   _____

   _____

   _____

Name: _____ Date: _____

Summary Exercise

A. Read the following paragraph, which contains short, choppy sentences. Use coordination and subordination to combine sentences and make the writing more effective.

College graduates can expect to earn at least $10,000 more annually than nongraduates. This is a good incentive for the college-bound. Someone has to pay for the expense of college. Financial aid will help some students. Only half of the students will receive federal, state, private, or school-financed assistance. Many students must study at public institutions. They cannot afford to go to private colleges and universities. Parents will have to pay most of the college costs. They will have to take out private loans. They will have to take second jobs to defray the costs. Sometimes students must take the responsibility for college tuition fees. They work part time to make ends meet.

B. Look at a paper you are working on, and notice your use of coordination and subordination. Revise to make sure that you are using both coordination and subordination and that you are using different sentence types.

CHECKING SPELLING, PUNCTUATION, AND MECHANICS

CHAPTER

29

29
spell

Strategies for Spelling

Consider the fact that the sounds in the word *see* (an *s* and an *e*) can be spelled in at least a dozen different ways, as illustrated in the words *see, senile, sea, scenic, ceiling, cedar, juicy, glossy, sexy, cease, seize,* and *situ.* Or consider the six different pronunciations of the letters *ough* in the words *cough, tough, bough, through, though,* and *thoroughfare.* English spelling is often difficult, and unless you have been gifted with a marvelous visual memory for the way words are spelled, the best you can do is to develop some practical strategies for identifying spelling problems and choosing correct spellings.

Spelling errors are most likely to occur as you draft. You can deal with them immediately, during drafting, or later, as you edit and proofread. If correct spelling is hard for you, try to keep this difficulty from turning into a fear of misspelling that distracts you from what you are trying to write. Worrying about spelling can draw your attention away from the most important parts of drafting and revising—exploring ideas and expressing them in effective ways. Stopping to check every word you *might* have misspelled is a sure way to disrupt your train of thought.

Giving special attention to spelling is therefore something often best reserved for proofreading. Nonetheless, you can take some positive steps to deal with spelling errors as you write. To recognize possible spelling errors as you draft, consider the following sources of incorrect spelling.

Inattention. You know the correct spelling of a word, but you don't use it. You might make a typing mistake. You might focus so hard on what you want to say or how to say it that you let a misspelling creep in. Usually, you can recognize errors of this sort quickly when you glance back over what you have written.

217

Guessing. You don't know the correct spelling of a word, so you guess on the basis of reason or of similar-sounding words. You know, for example, that the words *irreconcilable, reasonable, honorable, justifiable,* and *probable* all end with *-able,* so you reason that the word you don't know, *irresistible,* must do the same—and you get it wrong.

"Sounding Out." You don't know the correct spelling of a word, so you "sound it out." Although this strategy works occasionally, it can often lead you astray because of the sound/spelling discrepancies in English. And if you mispronounce a word, your spelling will probably be wrong. Many a motel billboard has mistakenly offered "congradulations" to a graduating class. Perhaps the most common spelling error in the United States is the infamous *alot,* incorrectly spelled as one word because, when spoken, the *a* and the *lot* blend together. Sounding out a word can be helpful during the drafting process, when you need to get the word down on the page and can't, for the moment, look it up. Nonetheless, you can recognize right away that the spelling *might* be wrong.

Instead of interrupting your thoughts to check every possible spelling error while you draft, simply circle the possible misspellings as you write. Come back to the circled words later, after you have completed drafting, and check them for misspellings. As you edit and proofread, you can use one or more of the following methods to recognize and correct misspellings.

Common patterns of misspelling

Many words contain groups of letters that can trip up even the best spellers. Other words have plural or compound forms that may be confusing, and others add suffixes and prefixes that need special attention.

Plurals. For most words, you can form a plural simply by adding *-s* (*novel, novels; experiment, experiments; contract, contracts*). Watch out for words that end in *-o* preceded by a consonant; they often add *-es* for the plural.

ADD *-ES*	potato, potatoes	tomato, tomatoes
	hero, heroes	zero, zeroes
ADD *-S*	cello, cellos	memo, memos

When a vowel comes before the *-o,* add *-s.*

ADD *-S*	stereo, stereos	video, videos

For words ending in a consonant plus *-y,* change *y* to *i* and add *-es.*

etiology, etiologies   gallery, galleries   notary, notaries

EXCEPTION	Add *-s* for proper nouns (*Kennedy, Kennedys; Tanury, Tanurys*).

For words ending in a vowel plus *y,* however, keep the *y* and add *-s.*

day, days   journey, journeys   pulley, pulleys

For words ending in *-f* or *-fe,* you often change *f* to *v* and add *-s* or *-es.*

hoof, hooves   knife, knives   life, lives   self, selves

Remember, however, that some words simply add -s.

> belief, beliefs   roof, roofs   turf, turfs

Words ending with a hiss (-*ch*, -*s*, -*ss*, -*sh*, -*x*, or -*z*) generally add -*es*.

> bench, benches   bus, buses   bush, bushes
> buzz, buzzes   fox, foxes   kiss, kisses

A number of one-syllable words ending in -*s* or -*z* double the final consonant: *quiz, quizzes*.

Though most plurals follow these simple rules, some do not, and you need to be alert for their irregular forms. Words with foreign roots often follow the patterns of the original language, as is the case with the following words drawn from Latin and Greek.

> alumna, alumnae (female)   criterion, criteria
> alumnus, alumni (male)   datum, data
> bacterium, bacteria   vertebra, vertebrae

Some familiar words form irregular plurals: *foot, feet; woman, women; mouse, mice; man, men.* (If you suspect that a word has an irregular plural, be sure to check a dictionary for its form.)

For compound words, use the plural form of the last word except in those few cases where the first word is clearly the most important.

> basketball, basketballs   pegboard, pegboards
> meadowland, meadowlands snowflake, snowflakes

EXCEPTION   sister-in-law, sisters-in-law

Word Beginnings and Endings. **Prefixes** do not change the spelling of the root word that follows.

> precut   post-traumatic   misspell   unendurable

The prefixes *in-* and *im-* have the same meaning, but you should use *im-* before the letters *b, m,* and *p.*

USE *IN-*   incorrect   inadequate   incumbent

USE *IM-*   immobile   impatient   imbalance

Suffixes may change the spelling of the root word that comes before, and they may pose spelling problems in themselves.

Retain the silent -*e* at the end of a word when you add a suffix beginning with a consonant.

KEEP -*E*   fate, fateful   gentle, gentleness

EXCEPTIONS   words like *judgment, argument, truly,* and *ninth*

Drop the silent -*e* when you add a suffix beginning with a vowel.

DROP -*E*   imagine, imaginary   generate, generation
                 decrease, decreasing   define, definable

EXCEPTIONS   words like *noticeable* and *changeable*

Four familiar words end in *-ery: stationery* (paper), *cemetery, monastery, millinery.* Most others end in *-ary: stationary* (fixed in place), *secretary, primary, military,* and *culinary.*

Most words with a final "seed" sound end in *-cede: precede, recede,* and *intercede,* for example. Only three are spelled *-ceed: proceed, succeed,* and *exceed.* One is spelled *-sede: supersede.*

The endings *-able* and *-ible* are easy to confuse because they sound alike. Add *-able* to words that can stand on their own and *-ible* to word roots that cannot stand on their own.

USE -*ABLE*   charitable, habitable, advisable, mendable
         Drop the e for word roots ending in one e (*comparable, detestable*), but keep it for words ending in double e (*agreeable*).

USE -*IBLE*   credible, irreducible, frangible

Adding the *-ed* and *-ing* endings

If a one-syllable word follows the pattern consonant-vowel-consonant, double the last consonant and add the ending.

DOUBLE CONSONANT	tip	tipped	tipping
	map	mapped	mapping

If a one-syllable word follows the pattern consonant-vowel-vowel-consonant, just add the ending.

ADD ENDING	dream	dreamed	dreaming
	roam	roamed	roaming

If a word ends in two consonants, just add the ending.

ADD ENDING	start	started	starting
	last	lasted	lasting

If a word ends in *-e,* drop the *-e* and add the ending.

DROP -*E*	hope	hoped	hoping
	tire	tired	tiring

If a two-syllable word stresses the first syllable, just add the ending.

ADD ENDING	happen	happened	happening
	wonder	wondered	wondering

If a two-syllable word ending in a consonant stresses the second syllable, double the last letter and add the ending.

DOUBLE LAST LETTER	prefer	preferred	preferring
	occur	occurred	occurring

If a word ends in a vowel and *-y,* just add the ending.

ADD ENDING	enjoy	enjoyed	enjoying
	relay	relayed	relaying

If a word ends in *-y,* change the *y* to an *i* and then add the *-ed* ending. Just add the *-ing* ending.

CHANGE Y TO I	study	studied
	try	tried
ADD ENDING	studying	
	trying	

If a word ends in *-ie,* change the *ie* to *y* and add the *-ing* ending. Just add *-d* to form the *-ed* ending.

CHANGE IE TO Y	lie	lying
	die	dying
ADD ENDING	lied	
	died	

Words containing *ie* and *ei*. Here is an old rhyme that tells you when to use *ie* and *ei*.

> *I* before *e*
> Except after *c,*
> Or when sounding like *a*
> As in n*ei*ghbor and w*ei*gh.

Most words follow the rule.

USE IE	believe, thief, grief, friend, chief, field, niece
USE EI	receive, deceit, perceive, ceiling, conceited

There are some exceptions.

EXCEPTIONS	weird, seize, foreign, ancient, height, either, neither, their, leisure, forfeit

29
spell

221

Name: _____ Date: _____

Exercise 1

A. Write the correct plural form for the words in the following list.

1. motto _____   6. phenomenon _____

2. estuary _____   7. mother-in-law _____

3. chemistry _____   8. football _____

4. turkey _____   9. woman _____

5. life _____   10. studio _____

B. Add the prefix -*in*, or -*im*, or -*un* words in the following list.

1. _____ possible   6. _____ reliable

2. _____ helpful   7. _____ tolerable

3. _____ believable   8. _____ proper

4. _____ happy   9. _____ lucky

5. _____ perceptible   10. _____ appropriate

C. Add the suffix -*ful*, -*able*, or -*ible* to the words in the following list. Make the necessary changes.

1. understand _____   6. define _____

2. believe _____   7. plenty _____

3. peace _____   8. hope _____

4. use _____   9. read _____

5. help _____   10. irrepress _____

D. Add -*ed* and -*ing* endings to the words in the following list.

1. stay _____ _____

2. weed _____ _____

3. hand _____ _____

4. dry _____ _____

5. type _____ _____

6. refer _____ _____

7. love _____ _____

8. abide _____ _____

9. study _____ _____

10. learn _____ _____

Commonly misspelled words

Words that sound like each other but are spelled differently (*accept/except, assent/ascent*) are known as **homophones.** Writers often confuse them, creating errors in both spelling and meaning.

INCORRECT   The city will not **except** any late bids for the project.

PROOFREAD   The city will not **accept** any late bids for the project.

The following list of homophones and other words often confused is designed to help you recognize errors in spelling or meaning as you proofread.

Commonly Misspelled or Confused Word Pairs

WORD	MEANING	WORD	MEANING	WORD	MEANING
accept	receive	cite	quote an authority	heard	past tense of *hear*
except	other than	sight	ability to see; a view	herd	group of animals
affect	to influence; an emotional response	site	a place	hole	opening
effect	result	complement	to complete or supplement	whole	complete
all ready	prepared	compliment	to praise	its	possessive form of *it*
already	by this time	desert	abandon	it's	contraction for *it is*
allusion	indirect reference	dessert	sweet course at conclusion of meal	later	following in time
illusion	faulty belief or perception			latter	last in a series
ascent	upward movement	discreet	tactful, reserved	lessen	make less
assent	agreement	discrete	separate or distinct	lesson	something learned
assure	state positively	elicit	draw out, evoke	meat	flesh
ensure	make certain	illicit	illegal	meet	encounter
insure	indemnify	eminent	well known, respected	loose	not tight
bare	naked	immanent	inherent	lose	misplace
bear	carry; an animal	imminent	about to happen	no	negative
board	get on; flat piece of wood	fair	lovely; light-colored; just	know	understand or be aware of
bored	not interested	fare	fee for transportation	passed	past tense of *pass*
brake	stop	forth	forward	past	after; events occurring at a prior time
break	shatter, destroy; a gap; a pause	fourth	after *third*		
capital	seat of government; monetary resources	gorilla	an ape		
		guerrilla	kind of soldier or warfare		
capitol	building that houses government	hear	perceive sound		
		here	in this place		

Exercise 2

Read the following sentences, and choose the correct word in parentheses.

EXAMPLE   Our chemistry professor is fond of giving (*a lot*, *alot*) of homework.

1. The teen club was created to keep the youngsters from getting (*bored*, *board*) after school.

2. The traditional (*role*, *roll*) of the mother in the family is that of caretaker.

3. People formerly (*though*, *thought*) that high cholesterol was due only to diet.

4. The Caribbean is a popular resort area because the (*whether*, *weather*) is so predictable.

5. If you think about future generations, you will see a need to recycle and protect the (*enviroment*, *environment*).

6. It is important to not (*loose*, *lose*) sight of your reasons for (*studying*, *studing*) in the United States.

7. During (*passed*, *past*) years, life has lost (*alot*, *a lot*) of (*it's*, *its*) simplicity.

8. Each of us needs to (*accept*, *except*) the fact that sometimes our problems will seem overwhelming.

9. The rising cost of tuition has made entrance into certain universities (*quiet*, *quite*) difficult; many people cannot (*afford*, *effort*) the fees.

10. The gymnasium is the (*fasility*, *facility*) on campus we are most proud of.

Strategies to improve spelling

A dictionary will give you the correct spelling of a word, and it may even offer spelling advice. For ESL students it can be helpful to use a learner's monolingual dictionary, such as the *Oxford Student's Dictionary of American English* or the *Longman's Dictionary of American English*, a bilingual dictionary, or a standard monolingual dictionary. If you have a general idea of how a word is spelled, especially how it begins, you can usually locate it in a dictionary with a little looking around. If you know how a word sounds but are not sure about the spelling, you can use the lists of correspondences between sound and spelling that some dictionaries offer. If you still cannot find a word's spelling, you may wish to use a specialized dictionary for people who have considerable trouble with spelling. These dictionaries list words both under their correct spelling (*phantom*, for example) and under likely misspellings (*fantom*).

Get help

All writers make some spelling errors that they simply can't fix because they don't know the word is misspelled. If at all possible, ask members of a revision group to identify any spelling errors you haven't caught. But first clean up all the errors you already know, even if you simply circle the words to identify them as misspelled. If someone else finds any more misspellings in your paper, you have the chance not just to fix them before sending the paper on to its reader but also to learn the correct spellings along the way.

Using long-term strategies to improve your spelling

Improving your spelling more generally is like improving anything that develops slowly: you need to practice. Here are three useful ways to become a more effective speller.

Use memory devices and pronunciation aids

The use of **mnemonics** (memory aids) can greatly improve your spelling by reminding you of odd spelling conventions that don't correspond with pronunciation. In *Beyond the "SP" Label*, Patricia McAlexander, Ann Dobie, and Noel Gregg offer a number of memory aids, including the following.

> *All right* is spelled like *all wrong*.
> *A lot* is like *a little*.
> *Emigrant, immigrant:* An emigrant leaves; an immigrant comes in.
> *Separate: sep_a_rate* rates two *a*'s; there's a rat in *sep_a_rate*.

Use these as models to create memory aids of your own.

Read more and attend to spellings

Nothing boosts literacy (spelling included) so powerfully as reading. The more you read, the more likely you are to see words spelled correctly. When reading, keep a list of words you might use (and might otherwise misspell) someday. Focus consciously on words with difficult spellings (if you've been doing that in this chapter, you may already have learned the spelling of *mnemonic*).

Build your own speller

The most useful spelling aid should look like someone's personal telephone book: filled with names and numbers generally meaningless to other people. If you keep track of words you commonly misspell, perhaps in a little notebook or file, you'll find yourself looking up possible candidates for misspellings much more quickly. As you begin learning and remembering the correct spellings, you can cross some words off your list as you're adding new ones.

Exercise 3

A. Look at the list of words below, and with a group of students think of mnemonic devices to help remember the words.

1. thorough/through
2. affect/effect
3. than/then
4. accept/except
5. adandon/adundant

6. advise/advice
7. necessary
8. business
9. government
10. success

B. Build a notebook of your most often misspelled words, listing the correct spelling for each word and the reason for the spelling. Continue adding to this notebook, and refer to it often.

EXAMPLE

Misspelled	*Correction*	*Reason*
realisticly	*realistically*	*with -ic endings, add -ally*

1. _____ _____ _____

2. _____ _____ _____

3. _____ _____ _____

4. _____ _____ _____

5. _____ _____ _____

6. _____ _____ _____

7. _____ _____ _____

8. _____ _____ _____

9. _____ _____ _____

10. _____ _____ _____

C. Circle words in your own writing that you feel may be misspelled. Review the information in this chapter, and determine whether the words are actual errors. Finally, use a dictionary to resolve any questions.

Spelling and the computer

The personal computer has become for spelling what the hand-held calculator became in the 1970s for routine math. If you use a word processor, you've no doubt discovered the virtues of the spelling checker, a program that searches your document for misspellings and asks you whether they're correct.

Understand how spelling checkers work

Most spelling checkers on personal computers work in conjunction with a dictionary that must be present in the computer's memory. Often these computer dictionaries hold several thousand basic words. When you ask the computer to screen your document for any spelling errors, it compares each word in your text with the words in the dictionary. If the word matches a word in the dictionary, the computer assumes the word is correctly spelled, and it moves on to the next word.

When the computer encounters a word that does *not* match any word in its dictionary, it asks you whether the word is misspelled. If it is, you can select an alternative spelling or type in the correction, and the computer then moves on until it finds the next possible error. A typical program also allows you to add words to its often limited dictionary. In this way, you can personalize the dictionary so that an unusual word or technical term won't be flagged every time the computer finds it in your paper.

Use a spelling checker cautiously

Using a spelling checker, especially on longer documents, is likely to reveal at least one or two errors. But whatever you do, don't rely *entirely* on a spelling checker to fix your writing.

A spelling checker can't reveal words that are properly spelled but used incorrectly. If it runs across the sentence "The Lakewood High quarterback lead his team to victory in the semifinals," a spelling checker will ignore *lead* because this is a correctly spelled word in the dictionary. But here, *lead* should be *led*.

The computer may flag a word as misspelled and then, on command, offer you other correct spelling options. If you're not careful, you can mistakenly choose the wrong word to be inserted in place of the misspelled one.

Editing Student Writing for Punctuation, Spelling, and Capitalization

As the final step in your drafting process, it is necessary to edit and proofread your writing for spelling, punctuation, capitalization, and other mechanical errors. You may want to review this material in earlier workbook chapters.

30
edit

Name: _____ Date: _____

Exercise 1

Edit the following paragraphs for mechanical errors. Look at punctuation, spelling, and capitalization.

A.

My future wife must have three caracterstics

Marriage is one of the most important decisions we make in our lives. I think the reason is that we are not meant to live alone. When I get marryed my wife must have three characteristics a compromising attitude an intelligent mind and a smile.

A compromising attitude will give people a good relationship. Marriage is a relationship that may last for thirty years or more. Although I can't promise that I won't fight at all with my wife over the years I will certainly try to make compromises. Sometimes couples can't get along and if we treet each other with a kind attitude we will work it out peacefully.

We are living in a society that is very complex and decisions have to be made all the time. We can't always know the right answer to our problems but if my wife is intelligent she can be a great help to me. We can share our knowledge of the world and live an intelligent life together.

I think the most beautiful thing is a smile. Whenever I glance at someone's smile I feel comfortable as if I have been blessed. A smile that comes from the heart brings a feeling of kindness. I would love to see the smile of my wife whenever I come home or wherever I am. I would forget all sorts of stress from life work and so on.

A compromising spirit, an intelligent attitude and a beautiful smile are the qualitys I want in my future spouse. Do you have any idea what else I need?

—Kyung-Jun Pak, College Student

B.

Traditional Festivity

Chinese New Year is the most important and meaningful festivity for all Chinese poeple. All Chinese people believe that the coming of the new year means changeing the old things for the new, and also changeing the bad things for the good. Therefore all people will treasure that day's coming and they will celebrate it.

New year is a busy time for all chinese people especially women who have to clean the house and prepare the food for the new year. Everybody hopes to live in happyer conditions in the new year. When the women clean the dirt out of the house they hope to clean out the bad luck as well.

New year is a time for people to have a delicious meal and be together with all the family. The New year dinner which is prepared and eaten on New Year's eve is one very important part of the celebrateion, because it is the last meal of the old year. According to Chinese tradition the whole family must gather together and enjoy the pleasure of a happy home circle. After the family finishs the dinner everybody gets dressed up in new clothing.

Chinese New Year is also very much a holiday for childs. Because they get to eat delicious food and dress up in new clothing children choose this holiday as their favorite holiday. In addition, parents and marryed relatives give children "lucky money" which is put in little red pouches. Finally children are given more freedom during the new year holiday and their parents rarly punish them at this time.

—Lai Ching Kong, College Student

C.

Freedom for Catalonia

Catalonia is a very small country, it is older than the United States, and it has been invaded many times. The last time was in 1936 when my grandfathers were between twenty and thirty years old, and my father was only six months old. The army of Spain had invaded Catalonia and there was a war for two years. During these two years, a lot of Catalan people were executed the Catalon language was forbiden, and the King of Spain was exiled. The president of Catalonia scaped to France, and General Francisco Franco established a dictatorship.

One of my grandfathers was in prison for a very long time but they didn't execut him because he knew alot of people. Both of my grandfathers are obsessed about the war and they often explain the historis of that time. General Franco died when I was seven years old, and now there is a democracy in Spain Catalonia is not a free country yet, but we have our own government and presedent.

—Marcel Centellas, College Student

D.

The United States

I would like to write a paragraph about a country where I live work and study. In America I see a country of opportunity, and education. America is a country of freedom, it is a country where everything is possibol. My major is biologi and in the future, I would like to study medecine. In my view, the United States is one of the best countrys in which to study medicine and this is conected to the excellent medical technologi in this country. I was surprised when I saw all the machines people were useing. Medicine in America is strong and powerful. We live in a country that has a great future.

—Markian Zaiats, College Student

Answer Key

Chapter 1: Articles

Exercise 1a

1. X, the, the
2. X, the
3. The, X
4. X, X, the
5. The, the, X

Exercise 1b

Students practice writing using articles and proper nouns.

Exercise 2a

1. The, a
2. X, the, a
3. X, X
4. the
5. The, X, the, the
6. The, a, the, a, a
7. The, the, X
8. the, X, X
9. X, X, the, the
10. X, an, the

Exercise 2b

Students practice using articles with singular and plural countable nouns.

Exercise 3a

1. X, the
2. X, X, the
3. X, X
4. the, X
5. the, X, X

Exercise 3b

Students practice writing using articles and uncountable nouns.

Exercise 4a

Culture Shock

Social scientists use **the** term culture shock for feelings of depression and homesickness that foreign students sometimes feel when they first live in **a** new country. Culture shock occurs because **a** student must adjust to **a** new language, unfamiliar foods, different behaviors, and unusual surroundings. There are three stages that accompany **the** experience of adjustment. During **the** first stage, **a** student may experience disbelief and shock. In **the** second stage, **a** student may feel despair and homesickness. Finally, in **the** third stage, **the** newcomer has **a** more hopeful and positive attitude. He or she begins to have **a** greater sense of identification with **the** new country. Once culture shock is recognized, symptoms of confusion and disorientation are diffused. It is also helpful to remind students that many others are feeling similar discomfort.

Proper Nouns	Singular, Countable	Plural, Countable	Uncountable
culture shock	term	scientists	depression
	country	feelings	homesickness
	student	students	disbelief
	language	behaviors	despair
	experience	surroundings	foods
	adjustment	stages	identification
	stage	symptoms	confusion
	shock	others	disorientation
	newcomer		discomfort
	attitude		
	sense		

A Korean Fable

Once upon **a** time in **the** countryside of Korea, there were **a** father and **a** daughter. They were living in poverty, and **the** father couldn't make **a** salary because he was blind. Only **the** daughter could get **a** small amount of money. During this time, **the** weather was very dry, and it had not rained for **a** long time. Therefore, **the** people of **the** town were looking for **a** young woman to sacrifice her life to **the** Dragon God in order to get rain. **The** daughter decided to volunteer because if she did, there would be money for her father. One day she jumped into **the** sea from **a** ship. From that time it rained for many days, and people could start farming. Her father was able to live in much richer circumstances than before, but he was very sad because his daughter had died. In **the** sea, **the** Dragon God was very impressed with **the** daughter's filial duty for her father. He decided to send her back to **the** earthly life with treasures. When **the** father saw his daughter again, he was filled with joy. Her name was Simchung, and today, when there is **a** person with great filial duty for parents, **the** Korean people call **the** person Simchung.

Proper Nouns	Singular, Countable	Plural, Countable	Uncountable
Korea	fable	people	poverty
Dragon God	time	days	money
	father	circumstances	time
	daughter	treasures	weather
	salary	parents	rain
	town		countryside
	woman		
	life		
	day		
	sea		
	ship		
	duty		
	joy		
	person		

Exercise 4b

Students work together to identify types of nouns and appropriate articles.

Exercise 4c

Students use their own writing to practice article usage.

Chapter 2: Adjectives

Exercise 1a

Answers will vary. Here are some possibilities.

1. Deep-sea diving is an **exciting** adventure for **daring** people of all ages.
2. The **modern** invention of **useful** scuba gear made **deep-sea** diving possible for **interested** people.
3. Some **adventurous** people become **successful** commercial divers.
4. Other **vacationing** divers dive for the **simple** pleasure of observing **fascinating** wildlife.
5. Divers can study **beautiful** water life and explore **sunken** ships.

Exercise 1b

A Night Dream

As I walk along the **white** beaches of my lovely land, I am swept away by the beautiful scenery. The **moody** waters of the sea come to the shore, always changing the **perfect** patterns. The **maternal** breezes hold me in quiet arms, and I am home again. I don't recognize any people on the beach, but their **strong** faces are somehow known to me. The precious sounds of my language are heard as a soothing Spanish song. I am walking in a familiar mist. Suddenly the wind picks up, and the solitude is broken. What are these **loud** noises I hear? Can the **ocean** winds make such sounds? Am I hearing a siren on the beach?

My alarm has sounded, and another day in the busiest city in the world begins. New York, you woke me up.

Exercise 1c

Answers will vary. Here are some possibilities.

1. rushing
2. crowded
3. yellow
4. tall
5. scenic
6. narrow
7. convenient
8. expensive
9. educational
10. luxury

Exercise 1d

Students practice using adjectives correctly in descriptive writing.

Chapter 3: Prepositions

Exercise 1a

1. John F. Kennedy was assassinated **in** Dallas **on** November 22, 1963.

2. A British passenger ship, the Titanic, hit an iceberg **on** April 14, 1912.

3. Alexei Leonov, a Soviet cosmonaut, first walked **in** space **in** 1965 **on** March 18.

4. Thomas Edison demonstrated the first incandescent lamp **in** New York City **on** October 21, 1879.

5. Hirohito became the emperor **of** Japan **in** 1926.

Exercise 1b
Students practice writing sentences using prepositions.

Exercise 2a

1. for
2. since
3. for
4. since
5. since

6. for
7. since
8. since
9. for
10. since

Exercise 2b
Students practice writing sentences using *for* and *since*.

Exercise 2c
Students interview one another. They then write a paragraph using *for* and *since*.

Exercise 3a
Circled answers are shown below in boldface type.

Music Is a Universal Language

People all over the world have a strong **appreciation of** music. A **love of** music has been the **reason for** many musical performances in many different countries. The **need for** music in our lives is very important no matter which country we are in. Throughout the year people **look forward to** classical recitals, jazz festivals, and rock concerts. It is definitely true that people of all ages have a **fondness for** music because music is ageless and timeless. It is also often true that people in every generation enjoy the music they are **familiar with,** but sometimes they are **interested in** new forms of music. Furthermore, people in different countries are **proud of** the rich musical heritage that is **particular to** their origins. Nonetheless, people can have a **respect for** and an **understanding of** the music of all different countries. Indeed, music is the universal language.

Exercise 3b

Noun + Preposition	Verb + Preposition	Adjective + Preposition
appreciation of	look forward to	familiar with
love of	interested in	proud of
reason for		
need for		
fondness for		
respect for		
understanding of		

Exercise 3c

Students choose noun-, verb-, or adjective-plus-preposition combinations and practice using these forms in writing.

Exercise 3d

Students have further practice with noun-, verb-, or adjective-plus-preposition combinations in freewriting.

Summary Exercise

I Often Think **About** My Native Country

While I was living **in** El Salvador, I had wonderful experiences. I often went **to** my favorite places; I am reminded **of** these places **in** my daily life **in** the United States. Sometimes when I am resting **in** my room, I daydream **about** the days when I went **to** dances **with** my friends. When I go **to** the beaches here, I reminisce **about** the warm and wonderful sea **in** El Salvador. I really enjoy remembering all the adventures that I have had **in** my country. Perhaps I can go there soon, and then I will bring back **with** me more memorable experiences and souvenirs.

Chapter 4: Gerunds and Infinitives

Exercise 1a

Students write sentences using gerunds and infinitives.

Exercise 1b

1. to acquire; acquiring
2. to teach; teaching
3. to recognize, (to) follow; recognizing, following
4. to learn; learning
5. to adapt; adapting

Exercise 1c

Students write a paragraph practicing the use of gerunds and infinitives.

Exercise 2

Students write sentences using gerunds.

Exercise 3a

1. shopping
2. swimming
3. skiing
4. talking
5. walking
6. tending
7. playing
8. listening
9. going
10. eating

Exercise 3b

looking forward to **having**; spend time **traveling**; spend time **walking** and **enjoying**; spends time **smiling** and **relaxing**

Exercise 3c

Students write sentences with expressions that take gerunds.

Exercise 4

Students write sentences that contain infinitives or objects and infinitives.

Exercise 5a

Students finish sentences using adjective expressions followed by infinitives.

Exercise 5b

Students write their own sentences using adjective expressions followed by infinitives.

Summary Exercise a

Choosing a Major and Selecting a Profession

College students are always faced with the decision of **choosing** a major. For first-year students, of course, it is sometimes difficult **deciding; to decide** exactly which major they might want **to study.** During the first two years of college, students must take required courses. After the sophomore year, however, students are asked **to declare** a major, and it is at this time that students begin **specializing; to specialize** in the subject of their choosing. Thus, they need **to select** a major in a subject that interests them. Students must also consider **finding out** information about work in their field of interest. Advisors recommend **experiencing** fieldwork in the student's area of interest, and in some colleges they expect students **to participate** in this activity as a required part of the curriculum. Once students have had experience in the field in which they intend **to work,** they start **understanding; to understand** important facts about the professions they are choosing. They can also practice **performing** the tasks of the particular profession. Students are greatly encouraged **to benefit** from on-the-job training. This experience lets students **make** intelligent choices about their future careers.

Summary Exercise b

Students practice using gerund and infinitive forms given in the chapter.

Summary Exercise c

Students have further practice with the gerund and infinitive forms in freewriting.

Chapter 5: Adjective Clauses

Exercise 1a

1. R <u>who are living together</u>

2. R <u>who come from so many diverse backgrounds</u>

3. NR , who come from smaller families and are accustomed to living in their own space,

4. NR , which discuss subjects like TV and study habits and attitudes toward budgets and guests,

5. R where students of similar educational and social interests can live together

6. NR , in which students of common interests live together,

7. R where students are immersed in a foreign language

8. NR which is in Long Beach, California,

9. NR , where many foreign students and Americans live,

10. R that focus on such themes as fields of study, health, and spirituality

Exercise 1b

Students write sentences with restrictive or nonrestrictive clauses.

Exercise 2a

1. Native American groups, **which** have distinct languages and cultures, represent an important part of U.S. history.

2. Geronimo was an Apache leader **who** was born in 1829 and died in 1909.

3. He was called Goyathlay, **which** means "one who yawns" in Apache.

4. Geronimo, **who** wanted to defend his people against white encroachment on Apache land, conducted many raids against both Mexican and American settlements in the Southwest.

5. History remembers another great tribe **that** was called the Cheyenne.

6. The Cheyenne tribe, **who** called their leader Chief Wolf Robe, were great warriors.

7. The Cheyenne were famous hunters **who** lived on the Great Plains.

8. They later settled on the Cheyenne River of North Dakota, **which** is named after the Cheyenne tribe.

9. The Cheyenne, **who** later helped to defeat General George Custer at the Battle of the Little Bighorn, formed an alliance with other tribes.

10. These people, **who** were from various tribes, witnessed the disappearance of both the buffalo and the wild frontier during their lifetimes.

Exercise 2b

Students write sentences with adjective clauses replacing subject pronouns.

Exercise 3a

1. In the 1800s many Americans were looking for a new life, **which** they believed could be found in the lands of the West.

2. Many Americans wanted the chance to own land, **which** they desired for farming.

3. By 1830, some lands in Mexico were settled by twenty thousand new people **whom** the Mexican government considered Mexican.

4. These new settlers, **whom** the Mexican government tried to control, continued to farm the lands of the Mexican territories.

5. Stephen Austin, **whom** the Mexicans threw into prison, went to Mexico City to discuss the problem.

6. The new Texans revolted against the Mexican government and took over a fort, **which** a Mexican general later tried to rescue.

7. The Texans won the battle and defeated the Mexican general, **who** was then held captive.

8. The Texans won independence from the Mexican government, **which** they didn't want to obey.

9. Texas, **which** its citizens called the Lone Star State, became an independent nation.

10. Sam Houston, **whom** people remember for his brave leadership, became the first president of Texas.

Exercise 3b

Students write sentences with adjective clauses replacing object pronouns.

Exercise 4a

1. The Sioux are a group of Native Americans **whose** language is spoken in various dialects across the United States.

2. Sitting Bull was a great Sioux leader **whose** wisdom, bravery, and powers of healing are legendary.

3. In order to fight off hostile U.S. troops, Sitting Bull participated in a great battle **whose** name—the Battle of the Little Bighorn—is still famous today.

4. The Iroquois Nation is a union of Iroquois-speaking Native Americans **whose** tribes include the Seneca, Cayuga, Onondaga, Oneida, and Mohawk.

5. The union has an organization called the Grand Council, **whose** aim is both to unite individual members and to maintain autonomy for each tribe.

6. The Iroquois are remembered for the political organization of the Iroquois Nation, **whose** democratic principles may have influenced the writing of the U.S. Constitution.

7. Today the Navajo, **whose** numbers exceed 150,000, constitute the largest Native American tribe left in the United States.

8. The Navajo**,** **whose** traditional view of the world includes belief in both good and evil forces**,** have the best-preserved Native American culture in North America.

9. The Navajo artists create sand paintings **whose** symbolic powers are believed to cure sick people.

10. A photographer **whose** name was Edward S. Curtis preserved the heritage and immortalized the culture of Native Americans.

Exercise 4b

Students write sentences with adjective clauses replacing possessive pronouns.

Exercise 5a

1. Edward S. Curtis is famous for his photographs of Native Americans, **about whom** there was great curiosity in both the United States and Europe.

   . . . **whom** there was great curiosity **about** in both the United States and Europe.

2. Curtis and others took many photographs, **to which** Native Americans were often resistant.

   . . . **which** Native Americans were often resistant **to.**

3. Government officials wanted to document the Native Americans, **about whose** lives they had great interest.

   . . . **whose** lives they had great interest **about.**

4. Many photographers were interested in taking historical photographs, **for which** they traveled all over the West.

   . . . **which** they traveled all over the West **for.**

5. The photographers, **with whom** some Native Americans were willing to cooperate, were busy taking historical photographs.

   . . . **whom** some Native Americans were willing to cooperate **with**

6. Curtis documented the Native American culture quite accurately, **for which** he received a lot of praise.

   . . . **which** he received a lot of praise **for.**

7. The pictures educated people about the Native American way of life, **for which** viewers began to have a greater respect.

   . . . **which** viewers began to have a greater respect **for.**

8. During this period the Native Americans were seen as a threatened race, **for whom** other people began to have great sympathy.

   . . . **whom** other people began to have great sympathy **for.**

9. Without the photographs taken at this time, we would have lost much of the Native American heritage, **from which** we have learned so many things.

   . . . **which** we have learned so many things **from.**

10. The photographs of Native Americans leave a rich legacy, **for which** we are grateful.

    . . . **which** we are grateful **for.**

Exercise 5b

Students write sentences with adjective clauses replacing objects of prepositions.

Exercise 6a

1. The early English immigrants, **the first of <u>whom</u>** settled in Jamestown, Virginia, and in Plymouth, Massachusetts, were looking for a new way of life.

2. In the late 1600s, large numbers of immigrants were Germans, **many of <u>whom</u>** settled in Pennsylvania.

3. Scotch-Irish immigrants, **most of <u>whom</u>** settled in lands along the frontier, came to America in large numbers.

4. French Huguenots, **some of <u>whom</u>** settled in New York State, came to the New World to flee religious persecution.

5. People from many different nations, **each of <u>whom</u>** brought their own customs and ideas, came to America for a new life.

6. The early settlers, **the majority of <u>whom</u>** were farmers, struggled to survive.

7. The colonists, **many of <u>whom</u>** were already skilled workers, also lived in manufacturing towns, such as Philadelphia, New York, Boston, Newport, and Charleston.

8. The early settlers, **most of <u>whose</u>** children were needed to help work, had large families.

9. Education was not always available to the early settlers, **few of <u>whom</u>** were ever formally educated.

10. People came to America looking for rights, **most of <u>which</u>** were religious, social, and civil freedoms.

Exercise 6b

Students write sentences with adjective clauses replacing objects of quantifiers.

Exercise 7a

1. which were built for the great pharaohs

   built for the great pharaohs

2. who were needed to build these mysterious monuments

   needed to build these mysterious monuments

3. that was achieved by Egyptian architects

   achieved by Egyptian architects

4. which originated in Central and South America and in Mexico

   originating in Central and South America and in Mexico

5. which still stands near Mexico City

   still standing near Mexico City

6. which is located in central Mexico

   located in central Mexico

7. that ornament the inside of the temple

   ornamenting the inside of the temple

8. which remind us of the great wisdom of ancient peoples

   reminding us of the great wisdom of ancient peoples

Exercise 7b

Students look through Exercises 1, 2, and 3 and determine whether adjective clauses can be changed to phrases.

Summary Exercise a

Con-Son, A Beautiful Island of Vietnam

Vietnam, which is a small country in Southeast Asia, is shaped like the letter *S*. With a long stretch of seashore on the Pacific Ocean, it has many beautiful beaches and islands. One of the most beautiful and important islands is Con-Son.

Con-Son is located southwest of Saigon, which is the capital of Vietnam. Forty miles away from the shore, Con-Son is surrounded by clear water and fine sand beaches. There is an abundance of coconut trees that were planted by prisoners who were kept there in the eighteenth century. Visitors who wish to experience this wonderful tropical island can come by plane or boat. Visitors who come by boat will have a chance to see a spectacular tunnel gate whose shap is formed by thousands of coconut trees and wildflowers. After traveling through this natural gate, the boat docks at Bai-Dam beach, where passengers can look through the light blue water and see a large array of fish that are dancing in the sea.

On top of a mountain on the island there is a lighthouse that was built by the French government when Vietnam was a French colony. During the war between the South and the North of the country, Con-Son was an island to which political prisoners were sent. Some have chosen to stay on as residents of this magical island. The sounds of coconut leaves that move in the air and waves that hit the shore make Con-Son a tropical paradise.

Summary Exercise b

Eleanor Roosevelt, An Outstanding First Lady

Eleanor Roosevelt, **who** was the wife of Franklin D. Roosevelt, the thirty-second president of the United States, was born on October 11, 1884, and died on November 7, 1962.

Eleanor Roosevelt, **who** was one of the most active first ladies of the twentieth century, was a strong advocate of humanitarian causes, **which** included employment of youth and civil rights for African Americans and women. In 1905 Eleanor married Franklin, **who** was her cousin. They had six children, one of **whom** died as an infant.

Eleanor Roosevelt, **who** is remembered as a highly gifted and energetic woman, expanded the role of first lady, **which** was traditionally limited. She was a tireless advocate for the underprivileged and for minorities. Eleanor, **who** was one of the most outspoken women in American public life, worked to improve education and international understanding. Throughout her life Eleanor continued to fight for the human rights in **which** she so strongly believed. The United Nations *Declaration of Human Rights*, **which** promised a dignified and secure future for all people, was adopted on December 10, 1948, in large part because of the personal and political vision of Eleanor Roosevelt, **who** was the U.S. representative to the UN at that time.

Eleanor Roosevelt was an extraordinarily active first lady during **whose** lifetime many important achievements were made for a better world.

Summary Exercise c

Students write a paragraph and practice using adjective clauses.

Summary Exercise d

Students work on adding adjective clauses to a paper in progress.

Chapter 6: Adverb Clauses

Exercise 1a

1. The number of foreign students studying in the United States is steadily increasing <u>because studying abroad gives them many new life experiences</u>.

2. This experience can present many dilemmas for students <u>as they are challenged by speaking and studying in a new language</u>.

3. <u>When students first start to speak in English</u>, they often feel uncomfortable and inhibited.

4. <u>Since the difficulties of communicating in a second language can be daunting</u>, foreign students sometimes choose to spend time with those who speak their own language.

5. However, <u>if foreign students wish to improve their English</u>, they should try not only socializing with native English speakers but also joining in the activities of a school club.

Exercise 1b

Americans Should Buy American

<u>Since I came to the United States</u>, I have often noticed that there are many Japanese cars in this country. It would be a better idea for Americans to buy cars made in America <u>because this would solve the growing problem of unemployment in the country</u>, and it might even improve the balance of trade between Japan and the United States. <u>When American car manufacturers began to produce smaller, better designed, better built, and more economical cars a few years ago</u>, it became practical for American consumers to buy American automobiles. <u>As soon as American people begin to realize the importance of buying American products</u>, they will help the country's economic problems and maybe even improve relations between Japan and the United States as well.

Exercise 2a

1. **Whenever** I leave New York City, I go directly to the subway station.

2. **After** I get to the subway station, I take the No. 1 train downtown.

3. I get off the subway car **as soon as** it gets to the 42nd Street stop.

4. **After** I get off at the 42nd Street subway station, I follow the signs to the Port Authority bus station.

5. **When** I arrive at the Port Authority, I go to the Adirondack Trailways desk to buy a round-trip ticket to upstate New York.

6. **Once** I purchase my round-trip ticket, I go downstairs to gate 33.

7. I make certain the bus is going to my town **before** I get on it.

8. **As soon as** the bus pulls into the station in my hometown, I see my parents waiting for me.

Exercise 2b

1. **Because** the temperature dropped to frigid levels, many problems have resulted.

2. **Since** the weather has gone way below the freezing point, everyone must dress in many layers of clothing and must always wear a hat and gloves.

3. Weather advisories are issued **because** people need to exercise extreme caution on the roads.

4. Motorists must leave for work an hour early **because** the roads have become very icy.

5. Some schools have been closed **because** their heating systems have been malfunctioning.

6. The grocery stores have often been crowded with customers **since** people have begun buying extra food in case of a snowstorm.

7. Utility companies are asking people to reduce their energy use **because** the frigid temperatures are raising demand for electricity.

8. Traveling has become difficult **since** the winter weather has arrived.

Exercise 2c

1. **Though** many people study the English language, it is not the most widely spoken language in the world.

2. **Although** Mandarin Chinese is the most widely spoken language in the world, many people choose to learn English instead.

3. In Switzerland four languages are spoken **although** the official language is French.

4. In Somalia only one language is spoken **whereas** more than a thousand different languages are spoken on the African continent.

5. In the United States we say that the toilet is in the bathroom, **but** in England it is in the water closet.

6. In Australia fried potatoes are called chips **whereas** in the United States they are called french fries.

7. **While** Esperanto is no longer a widely used language, it is estimated that it is spoken by some eight million people.

8. Germany has only one official language, called High German **although** there are numerous dialects throughout the country.

Exercise 2d

1. In some cultures you are considered rude **if** you look directly into the eyes of another person while talking.

2. In American culture you are considered rude **if** you do not look into the eyes of a person while talking.

3. In some cultures you are easily accepted when you are visiting **provided that** you remove your shoes when you are inside the home.

4. In American culture you don't need to remove shoes in the home **provided** you are visiting.

5. In some Hispanic cultures people stand very close to one another in conversation **because** they wish to communicate friendship.

6. **As long as** you maintain enough physical distance between yourself and a person you are talking to, in American culture people feel more comfortable.

7. In certain countries either a handshake or a bow is expected **whenever** people are meeting formally.

8. People need to learn unspoken behaviors of a new culture **even if** they know the language.

Summary Exercise a

Students finish sentences with a subordinator and an adverb clause.

Summary Exercise b

Students write sentences using adverb clauses of time, reason, contrast, and condition.

Summary Exercise c

Answers may vary. Here is one possible version.

Learning Japanese as a Second Language

As soon as we sat aboard a plane headed for Japan, my son and I began to study our *Speedy Japanese* book for beginners. We wanted to learn the numbers 1 to 10 in Japanese **before** we landed **because** we believed that this knowledge would help us **after** we arrived.

As we made our way through the crowded airport, the new sound of the language was strange and exciting. **As soon as** we saw our friend who was waiting for us, we felt more relaxed. She helped to translate signs for us and helped us to maneuver in this wonderful new country. **When** we got to her apartment, we wanted to sleep, **but** it was only 6 p.m.

The Japanese people were so patient and so friendly to us **whenever** we met them. **If** we needed help of any kind, they were always willing to give it. **When** we were feeling rather homesick, we went to a baseball game. It felt so good to see that familiar sport, **yet** the Japanese version of the game is a little different.

After spending a whole month in a new country, we felt almost strange arriving back at Kennedy Airport in New York. We had grown accustomed to hearing a language that we couldn't understand, **whereas** back in New York we suddenly were a part of the system. This is an experience you cannot fully understand **unless** you have traveled to a foreign land. We learned that **if** we wanted to continue our study of Japan and the Japanese people, we would have to return for many more months.

Summary Exercise d
Students develop a paragraph using adverb clauses.

Summary Exercise e
Students add adverb clauses to a paper in progress.

Chapter 7: Noun Clauses

Exercise 1a
1. It is a fact that there are many solar systems in the Milky Way.
2. How many other solar systems exist beyond our solar system is unknown.
3. It is also not known whether there is any form of life in these other solar systems.
4. Scientists continue to investigate how the universe began.
5. Many people believe that the universe is expanding; others think that it is contracting.
6. The big bang theory states that the universe began to expand from a single point billions of years ago.
7. Some versions of the theory suggest that many universes may have come into existence in much the same way.
8. It is also believed, however, that many galaxies are obscured from view.
9. Many people wonder, in fact, whether the number of galaxies may be infinite.
10. Because there may be millions of other solar systems in the universe, many people think that life must exist elsewhere.

Exercise 1b

The Importance of Work

It is true <u>that people need to work for many reasons</u> and <u>that they can profit from the experience</u>. Work has taught me <u>how to be assertive</u>, <u>how to be responsible</u>, and <u>how to be punctual</u>. Having a job taught me <u>that it is important to be able to communicate with superiors and other workers</u>. Formerly, I did not know <u>how to get along well with others</u>, but my work experience taught me this important lesson. <u>That people work well together in any job</u> is very necessary. I also learned <u>that I had a responsibility to others and not just to myself</u>. It was important <u>that I arrive at work on time</u> and <u>that I put forth my best effort</u>. <u>What I learned from my work experience</u> has been invaluable in teaching me life lessons.

Exercise 2a

1. Who is in the audience?
   Who is in the audience doesn't interest me.
   The television shows us **who is in the audience.**

2. Where are the secret service agents?
   Where the secret service agents are is difficult to see.
   It is difficult to see **where the secret service agents are.**

3. Where can I meet the president?
   Where I can meet the president is still unknown.
   It is still not known **where I can meet the president.**

4. When do you plan to introduce us?
   When you plan to introduce us is very important to me.
   It is very important to me **when you plan to introduce us.**

5. How has the president become so popular?
   How the president has become so popular is of great interest to me.
   I am greatly interested in **how the president has become so popular.**

Exercise 2b

Students create questions using *who, what, where, why, when, how,* and so on, then write the answers. In writing these answers, they will create noun clauses naturally.

Exercise 2c

1. Everyone realizes that space exploration has advantages and disadvantages.

2. It is understood that the cost and the benefits of space exploration are very high.

3. It is amazing that we have the technological know-how to develop rockets.

4. It cannot be denied that to be able to leave the earth's atmosphere and travel into space is an extraordinary accomplishment.

5. It is easily understood that people have always had a great interest in learning about the universe.

6. It is a fact that the Greek astronomer Eratosthenes measured the earth's size fairly accurately.

7. Copernicus was the first modern European to theorize that the earth orbits the sun.

8. In 1978 scientists discovered the fact that Pluto has one moon.

9. We now know that the two nearest galaxies are the Andromeda galaxy and the Magellanic Clouds.

10. It is true that people will always try to explore the unknown territories of both the planet and the sky above.

Summary Exercises a and b

Students develop paragraphs using noun clauses.

Summary Exercise c

Students identify or add noun clauses in a paper in progress.

Summary Exercise for Adjective, Adverb, and Noun Clauses

Albert Einstein

Albert Einstein, **who was born in Germany in 1879 and died in the United States in 1955,** contributed more than any other scientist to the world of the twentieth century. **It** is an interesting fact **that when Einstein was very young, he actually failed school examinations.** He graduated in 1900 as a teacher of mathematics and physics.

Einstein wrote three important papers on the subject of physics, **one of which was about quantum mechanics, which is a theory of physics concerned with electrons and light.** The second paper proposed the theory of relativity, **in which Einstein presented new and important ideas about energy and mass.** The third paper, **which involved statistical mechanics,** considered atomic motion.

Einstein's theory of relativity, **for which he is most remembered,** was a new way of looking at time, space, matter, and energy. He proved **that a small amount of matter can produce a large amount of energy.** Einstein left the world with many new theories of physics, **for which he won the Nobel Prize for Physics in 1921.** He believed **that there is a fundamental**

order to all of nature and that there is a unity of all humanity. For these reasons Einstein worked throughout his life to spread knowledge and world peace.

Chapter 8: Simple Present and Simple Past Tense

Exercise 1a

1. Our classmates **come** from five different countries.

2. Some students **originate** from Japan, China, and Korea.

3. Another student **represents** her country, Egypt.

4. Two other students **come** from Mexico.

5. Many students **hope** to graduate from a U.S. university.

6. Multinational students **communicate** with each other in the language they have in common, English.

7. An English as a Second Language class **teaches** everyone that the world is multilingual and multicultural.

Exercise 1b

1. Invisible vibrations **make** sound.

2. Sound is made by the vibration of objects, which **sends** waves through the air.

3. The number of the vibrations **makes** a difference; it **determines** the kind of sound we **hear.**

4. Sounds **can** be low, high, soft, or loud.

5. If an object **vibrates** many times per second, it **makes** a high-frequency sound.

6. High frequencies **make** high-pitched sounds.

7. Objects that **vibrate** very slowly **produce** low-frequency waves and **make** low-pitched sounds.

8. However, sound **does** travel very well under water.

9. Many creatures of the ocean **perceive** the vibrations of sound from great distances.

10. Sound **travels** more slowly than light; therefore, during electrical storms, the sound of the thunder **takes** longer to reach us than the sight of the lightning **does.**

Exercise 1c

Students write sentences, paying careful attention to the third person -s.

Exercise 2a

1. Correct
2. believe
3. offers
4. learn
5. Correct
6. consider, considered
7. appreciate, appreciated
8. have, had
9. Correct
10. agree

Exercise 2b

Students look at a paper in progress and identify the main verbs, checking to see that they are in a completed form.

Summary Exercise a

Students interview classmates and write about what they learn. They then edit their work for correct present tense verb endings.

Summary Exercise b

Students write their third person biographies and check the use of third person endings.

Summary Exercise c

A Typical Boy

Kit Fei Chan is a typical boy, just like many other boys who are born in Canton, China. His hometown is located in the countryside. Perhaps this place would not be preferable or attractive to city children because they would think it **lacks** fun and modern conveniences. However, for the children in the country, it is almost like a paradise. They enjoy swimming, jogging, and playing group games. Kit Fei **enjoys** these games, too.

When Kit Fei and his family **receive** a visa to emigrate to the United States, he **feels** so sad because he **knows** he is going to miss all his friends and relatives and the country roads he **loves** to walk on. As soon as Kit Fei **arrives** in New York, he **feels** very strange about the new and different environment. He **tries** very hard to adapt to his new life in America. He **enters** a bilingual school that **provides** him with many wonderful opportunities. He **overcomes** his difficulties, **makes** new friends, and **graduates** from high school.

Kit Fei **gets** accepted to an American college, and he **studies** very hard in order to achieve his goals. Through all his experiences he **learns** to meet the many challenges of life in a new country.

Chapter 9: Irregular Verbs

Exercise 1a

1. The weather forecaster **had chosen** to alert the television viewers to the impending snow-storm.

2. All the major networks **had spoken** of the storm for many days prior to its arrival.

3. Despite the television coverage of the storm watch, the snow **had crept** into the area in the dead of night.

4. During the evening rush hour, commuters **had driven** without any problems, but in the morning, travel was impossible.

5. By early morning, people **had woken** up to find that the commute would be impossible.

6. Train service in and out of major cities **had fallen** behind schedule.

7. For one whole day, airplanes in area airports **had not flown.**

8. Twenty-four hours after the storm **had come** to the area, people **had forgotten** that spring was coming soon.

Exercise 1b

Students write sentences using irregular verbs correctly or incorrectly. Then they edit a partner's work.

Exercise 1c

Students identify and correct irregular verbs in their papers in progress.

Chapter 10: Verb Forms

Exercise 1a

My Last Year in High School

"I have never been so lost in my life before." These were my exact feelings when I graduated from high school. I was eighteen years old that year. I had become an adult, and my life had totally changed. I was going to be separated from my friends. I had to leave my high school whe I had spent so many years. I had to say good-bye to my friends and teachers to whom I had become very attached. I cried a lot about this because I didn't want to grow up and face my unknown future by myself. I graduated from high school more in sorrow than in happiness.

My sweet memories of high school are the only things which I can have to carry on. As time passes, I realize that I don't have to stay with my friends all the time because my friends will remain in my heart.

Exercise 1b

Students work together to identify main and helping verbs in their own papers.

Exercise 2a

1. We **were** forming an international students club last semester.

2. The president **is** planning many trips for international students this semester.

3. We **will be** going to Washington, D.C., with the club next semester.

4. Students **will be** visiting the United Nations in New York City in the fall of next year.

5. We **were** planning to go there last year, but we had no travel funds.

6. This semester we **are** budgeting our money more wisely.

Exercise 2b

Students write sentences using the past, present, and future progressive tenses to describe their activities.

Exercise 2c

1. The international students **had** begun to meet as a group over the summer before the semester started.

2. The club members **have** decided to meet every Thursday night this semester.

3. The students **will have** written the agenda for the coming semester before the next meeting.

4. Last semester the students **had** hoped to accomplish many things.

5. This semester the club **has** decided to be more realistic about its goals.

6. The club's travel plans **will have been** decided by the end of the first meeting.

Exercise 2d

Students write sentences using the past, present, and future perfect tenses to describe their activities.

Summary Exercise a

1. Ali will have **finished** the TOEFL test by noon today.

2. He has **prepared** very carefully for the exam.

3. While he is taking the test, his father will **have** a bite to eat in the cafeteria.

4. Ali **was** feeling anxious about the exam late last night, but this morning he felt much better.

5. After he finishes the exam, he **is** planning to look for an apartment in town.

6. The dormitories have **been** full since last week, so he must rent a place off campus.

7. First, of course, he **will try** to find a newspaper.

8. His father will **help** him to locate an apartment.

9. Together they can **find** an apartment within walking distance of campus.

10. After that Ali's college life can begin.

Summary Exercise b

The New York City marathon **has** been a popular event for many years. Most of the runners **have been** training for many weeks before the event. The competitors **can** be any age from their early twenties to their eighties. The course for the runners **has** always been through the five boroughs of New York. Last weekend, the marathon racers began the race at noon in Central Park. It **was** raining the night before, but the race started anyway. Traffic **was** stopped in the park by barricades. The runners **were** feeling nervous as the time to start came closer. Some of them **had** not slept very well the night before. They **were** worrying about the race and thinking of the many weeks of training that they had **endured.** The television camera crews **were** aiming their cameras at the crowd. Each runner **was** hoping to win because each had **worked** very hard. The gun went off.

Summary Exercise c

Students check the verb forms in one of their own papers.

Chapter 11: Simple Present and Present Progressive

Exercise 1a

1. He **is** a single parent.

2. Every day he **manages** a very busy schedule.

3. Right now he **is finding** it helpful to talk to other people who **are coping** with the same difficulties as he is.

4. This semester he **is working** full time and **taking** (or **is taking**) one course at a local college.

5. Every week the children **follow** a list of chores to help in the house.

6. The list **hangs** on the refrigerator.

7. John **pays** the children a dollar for each job.

8. Every weekend he **goes** hiking or skiing in the nearby mountains with his children.

9. Now John **knows** how to juggle two jobs—housework and office work.

10. At the moment, John **is learning** to be a father, caretaker, and provider.

Exercise 1b

Students write about their families' habits, using simple present tense and frequency adverbs.

Exercise 1c

Students use the present progressive tense in writing about observations of behavior in different locations, such as the library, the cafeteria, or a classroom.

Exercise 1d

Students write ads for roommates, using correct simple present and present progressive forms.

Chapter 12: Simple Past and Present Perfect

Exercise 1a

Zoological Gardens

The first zoo **was** founded in China in the twelfth century. Wen, the ancient Chinese king who **started** it, **wanted** to collect exotic animals from all over his empire. He **kept** them in a garden which he **called** the Garden of Intelligence.

In ancient times many zoological collections also **existed** in Egypt and the Middle East. At that time wealthy people **kept** a great variety of wild animals for their personal collections.

During the eighteenth century, zoos **were** built in Vienna and Madrid, and zoos **became** open to the public. From that time to the present, people **have shown** an interest in visiting zoos for entertainment. In addition, they **have learned** many things about the animal world.

Although there are many notable zoos throughout the world, some of the largest zoos are in North America. They **were** built in the Bronx; New York City; Washington, D.C.; and San Diego. Zoos **have entertained** people for many years. Going to the zoo **has become** not only a recreational activity but also an educational one for families.

Since the middle of the twentieth century, the increasing human population **has destroyed** many animal habitats, thereby threatening the survival of certain animal species. Therefore, zoos **have become** places where endangered animal species can breed in protected areas.

Exercise 1b

Students practice using the simple past tense and the present perfect tense in sentences.

Exercise 1c

1. Kite flying <u>has been</u> a national pastime in some Asian countries for many centuries.

2. Chinese, Koreans, Japanese, and Malayans <u>have used</u> kites since approximately 1000 B.C.

3. In Asia people <u>believed</u> that kites would keep away evil spirits.

4. In China many people <u>have enjoyed</u> kite flying strictly for fun over the years, and they still do today.

5. In engineering, kites <u>have been used</u> to build bridges.

6. In meteorology, kites <u>have carried</u> weather recording instruments.

7. Kite-flying contests <u>started</u> long ago.

8. A kite-flying record <u>has been achieved</u> with a string of ten kites.

9. Kite flying <u>has been</u> popular along the seashore because of windy conditions.

10. In China the ninth day of the ninth month <u>has been designated</u> as Kite Day.

Exercise 1d

Students practice using the simple past and present perfect tenses in freewriting.

Chapter 13: Simple Past and Past Perfect

Exercise 1a

The Forcing

I <u>had been</u> so happy. I <u>had had</u> a world that totally <u>belonged</u> to me: my country, my friends, my familiar places, even the sky. They <u>had</u> all <u>been</u> reality to me. I <u>had had</u> my dream. I <u>had chosen</u> my goals. All these <u>had made up</u> a glorious picture—my childhood during the time I <u>was</u> in China. However, just as each sentence <u>has</u> a period to symbolize the end, my life <u>changed</u> abruptly in the same way.

This picture of my life suddenly <u>stopped</u> with the sound of the airplane engines. The plane <u>flew</u> higher and higher; my heart <u>said</u> good-bye again and again. I <u>had tried</u> to say good-bye to everyone in that picture before I <u>left</u>, but the faces <u>were</u> still in my mind.

At that time, my parents <u>were sitting</u> next to me, but I still <u>felt</u> alone. I <u>didn't want</u> to say anything to them. They <u>had changed</u> my life. I <u>knew</u> they <u>were bringing</u> me to the United States so that my brother and I <u>could have</u> good educational and career opportunities. But, on the other hand, they <u>had taken</u> my happiness away and <u>had pushed</u> me into a dark hole, traveling in the airplane toward the unknown. It <u>was</u> as if I <u>were</u> blind. I <u>was yelling</u>, "Where <u>is</u> the sky?" All I could think to myself was, "What is more important—education or happiness?" Also, I asked myself, "Do I have any choices?" The answer was, "No, absolutely not." I could only choose the United States because I could not live alone at fourteen years of age. I realized that I had already dropped happiness in China and had accepted sadness in the United States by the time I landed in the new country.

"Good-bye China . . ."

Exercise 1b

Students use the past perfect tense to write sentences about their activities before they came to the United States.

Exercise 1c

By using time expressions such as *by the time, when, before,* and *after,* students practice using the simple past and past perfect tenses.

Exercise 1d

Students use the simple past and past perfect tenses in writing sentences about the lives of other students.

Exercise 1e

Students use the simple past and past perfect tenses in writing about their own lives.

Chapter 14: Simple Present and Future Perfect Tenses, and Future Time Clauses

Exercise 1a

Students write sentences using the future perfect tense.

Exercise 1b

Students complete the sentence "By the time I return to my country . . ." and practice using the future perfect tense.

Exercise 1c

1. When my education **is finished,** my life **will have changed** in many ways.

2. By the time I **am finished** studying in the United States, I **will have learned** a new way of life.

3. I **will have received** my diploma before I **get** married.

4. I **will have gotten** a good job by the time I **have** children.

5. Before I **become** successful, I **will have worked** very hard in my profession.

Exercise 1d

Students write about the activities of classmates and practice using the simple present and future perfect tenses.

Exercise 1e

Students write about their plans for the future and practice using the simple present and future perfect tenses.

Chapter 15: Conditionals

Exercise 1a

Students complete sentences using Type I conditionals (general habit).

Exercise 1b

Students complete sentences using Type I conditionals (one-time event, true in the future).

Exercise 1c

Students complete sentences using Type I conditionals (one-time event, possibly true in the future).

Exercise 1d

Working in a group or with a partner, students write Type I conditional sentences to create a paragraph.

Exercise 2a

Students complete sentences using Type II conditionals (present untrue).

Exercise 2b

Working in a group or with a partner, students write Type II conditional sentences to create a paragraph.

Exercise 3a

Students complete sentences using Type III conditionals (past untrue).

Exercise 3b

Working in a group or with a partner, students write Type III conditional sentences to create a paragraph.

Exercise 4a

Life Without Electricity

We have much for which to thank Thomas Alva Edison, the great inventor of the nineteenth century, whose work with electricity changed the lives of all future generations. Life **would be** very different if it **were not** for the use of electricity. We **would live** a much simpler life in some ways if electricity **had not been invented** by Edison, and we **would have to** forgo many of life's conveniences. In fact, if suddenly we **tried** to live life without electricity, we **would find** that to do almost anything, we **would want** to use some form of electrical power. If it **were not** for electricity, we **would not have** some of the greatest inventions of the twentieth century, such as motors, generators, telephones, radio and television, and computers. Our world **would be** a darker and duller place without electricity, and the pace of living **would be** a lot slower. What **would** life **be** like?

Exercise 4b

Using a Common World Language

So many languages are spoken in the world. Different people speak different languages. The French speak French, the Chinese speak Chinese, and so on. If one common language were spoken in the world, it would serve as a bridge linking all countries together.

A common world language would help to keep world peace. The world is like a family, and the people who live in it should look upon each other as fathers, mothers, sisters, and brothers. As we know, if a family wants to live in harmony, it needs to have understanding among the family members. If a family wants to achieve understanding, its members must speak the same language. If the world family spoke a common language, there would be greater understanding among all people. If there were greater understanding, there would be fewer conflicts. If there were fewer conflicts, violence and wars would disappear.

In addition, if there were a common world language, difficulties for immigrants would be greatly reduced. I know this from my own experience. If I had been able to use a common language when I first came to the United States, my experience would have been much easier. I could have gone directly to college, and I might have worked successfully in an American company. For everyone, if we had a world language in common, what a wonderful life it would be!

Exercise 4c

Students practice writing using Type I conditional forms.

Exercise 4d

Students practice writing using Type II conditional forms.

Exercise 4e

Students practice writing using Type III conditional forms.

Chapter 16: Active and Passive Voice

Exercise 1a

1. is written
2. was written
3. will be written
4. has been written
5. is being written
6. had been written
7. was being written
8. is going to be written
9. will have been written
10. was discovered
11. had been discovered
12. will be discovered
13. has been discovered
14. is going to be discovered
15. will have been discovered
16. is discovered
17. was being discovered
18. is being discovered

Exercise 1b

1. said
2. has said
3. will say
4. is going to say
5. had said
6. is saying
7. was saying
8. will have said
9. is saying
10. told
11. is telling
12. had told
13. was telling
14. has told
15. told
16. will have told
17. is going to tell
18. will tell

Exercise 1c

1. Manufacturers produce sugar in many countries. [active]

2. People began the sugarcane culture in New Guinea. [active]

3. Sugarcane plants require a warm, moist climate. [active]

4. At harvest people using machetes or machines cut the sugarcane close to the ground. [active]

5. The leaves are stripped off the stalks, and the sugarcane is transported to a sugar mill. [passive]

6. At the sugar mill, cane juice is extracted from the stalks by machines. [passive]

7. Ships <u>transport</u> most raw sugar to refineries to be washed and crystallized. [active]

8. The familiar white sugar <u>is produced</u> by the refineries. [passive]

9. People <u>package</u> the sugar and <u>sell</u> it in stores. [active]

10. Throughout the world, sugar <u>is consumed</u> by many people in large quantities. [passive]

Exercise 2a

Students may have varying reasons for choosing to change to the passive voice.

1. Last Thursday a work of art was stolen from the Chicago Museum. (Passive is better—reason 1.)

2. The active sentence is better; the subject is important.

3. The active sentence is better; the subject is important.

4. Anyone who saw the thieves is being asked to contact the police investigation bureau. (Passive—reason 1)

5. As soon as the thieves are caught, they will be arrested. (Passive—reasons 1 and 3)

6. The painting will be sold on the black market. (Passive—reason 3)

7. Sometimes original paintings are reproduced illegally. (Passive—reason 2)

8. The reproductions are sold as original paintings. (Passive—reason 3)

9. Such acts of fraud must be stopped. (Passive—reason 5)

10. International governments have been alerted about this robbery. (Passive—reason 4)

Exercise 2b

Radon

Radon is an inert gas. Radon **was discovered** in 1900 by F. E. Dorn. This gas **was called** radium emanation. Since 1923 it **has been known** as radon, and it **has been given** the symbol Rn. Today, it **is believed** that nearly half of all the background radioactivity in the environment **is made up** of radon. Although radon **is found** in harmless quantities in many areas of the United States, some unsafe levels of radon **have been discovered** in homes throughout the country. This gas, which is called radon-222, **is produced** by the naturally occurring radium in the ground. Once it is present in the home, the gas **can be absorbed** into the lungs. It **is estimated** that annually 5,000 to 20,000 cases of lung cancer **are caused** by the presence of high quantities of radon in the home. The problem **can be alleviated** through ventilation systems, but they can be costly.

Exercise 2c

Students may have varying explanations for use of the passive voice in this exercise.

The Martial Arts

The martial arts, which come from Japan, Korea, and China, <u>were</u> once <u>used</u> only for self-defense. As little as fifty years ago, these defensive arts <u>were not</u> even <u>known</u> in the United States. Today, however, we know that great skill and many years of rigorous training <u>are required</u> to master these sports. Judo, aikido, and jiujitsu come to the United States from Japan. In 1964 judo <u>was accepted</u> as an official Olympic sport. In this sport, the opponent <u>must be pinned</u> and <u>held</u> on the mat for thirty seconds in order for the other player <u>to be declared</u> a winner. Aikido is another defensive art in which players attempt to unite the mind and the body to accomplish victory. Jiujitsu <u>is practiced</u> by the Japanese military. The opponent <u>is held</u> in a position through the combined leverage, strength, balance, timing, and speed of the winner. In this way victory <u>is achieved</u>.

Tae kwon do, which comes from Korea, and kung fu, which comes from China, are also very popular defensive arts in the United States.

Exercise 2d

Students practice using the active or passive voice in a writing activity.

Chapter 17: Verb Usage Review

Students will have varying explanations for the use of verb tenses. If students are uncertain, they should review the material in the verb chapters in this section.

Exercise 1a

came, felt, experienced, happened, saw, had never seen, had to learn, began to adapt, was, felt, lost, had already learned, want, is, read, am trying, am doing, have assimilated, am, haven't forgotten, believe, will have melted

Exercise 1b

were, wanted, was, came, suggested, should draw, is, will get, agreed, was, was going, started, finished, had not started, have, will draw, announced, am, handed, had finished, do not have, is not, explained, do, are asked, will spoil

Exercise 1c

is, will live, is, suits, will have, will have, will share, will have, will have, end, can work, will be able, will buy, will travel, must be, will return, will be, should do, gets, must be willing, do, will argue, will be, will have, is, can become, is, will make, will take away, do, doesn't like, will tell, will not be, will be, has, will be, will enjoy

Exercise 1d

hope, is coming, will be, will have become, will no longer need, will have been able, will no longer work, will work, will have arrived, will be, will be, will go, is

Chapter 18: Subject-Verb Agreement

Exercise 1a

1. am
2. have
3. is
4. are
5. are, am
6. have
7. are
8. is
9. has
10. is
11. is
12. has
13. has, has
14. are
15. have

Exercise 1b

Students practice using *be* and *have* in sentences about themselves or their families.

Exercise 1c

Students have further practice substituting pronouns in sentences.

Exercise 2a

1. Many parents do understand the behavior of teenagers.

   Many parents don't understand the behavior of teenagers.

2. To be effective, parents do need to remember their own youth.

   To be effective, parents don't need to remember their own youth.

3. A teenage child does require extra understanding and patience.

A teenage child doesn't require extra understanding and patience.

4. Some adolescents do respect the opinions of the older generation.

   Some adolescents don't respect the opinions of the older generation.

5. Certain young adults do sympathize with the concerns of parents.

   Certain young adults don't sympathize with the concerns of parents.

Exercise 2b

Students practice using emphasis or the negative in sentences.

Exercise 2c

Students practice using emphasis or the negative in a paragraph.

Summary Exercise a

Islam

S V Islam **is** a religion that was officially founded in A.D. 622. **S V** Islam is related to Judaism and **S V** Christianity. It **has** many followers, second in numbers only to those of the Christian faith. **S** Mohammed, the great prophet and leader of Islam, **V was** born 570 in Mecca in western Arabia. **S V** His followers **are** called Muslims, and **S V** they have many important codes of behavior that must be followed. **V** There **are S** four pillars of Islam: fasting for the holy month of Ramadan; praying five times a day; giving *zakat,* which are donations to the needy; and making a pilgrimage once in a lifetime to Mecca. **S V** Muslims **obey** the rules of Islam, and **S V** they **try** to follow a moral life. The **S V** rules of Islam **are** written in the holy book called the Koran. **S** Muslim people **V believe** in the integrity of all religions. **S** Today we still **V do** have the opportunity to visit many beautiful mosques built many years ago, and **S** we **V** are reminded of the beginnings of Islam.

Summary Exercise b

The Importance of Friendship

S V *Friend* is the most important word in my life. **S** This word **V means** a lot to me. **S V** I love to make friends, and since **S V** I am an active person, **S V** I am often the one who **initiates** a conversation with **S V** others. I can't stand loneliness; thus, **S** finding someone to share tears and laughter **V is** very important to me.

V In America it has been a painful experience for me **S** to be separated from my friends. Since I have been here, letters, cards, and packages from my friends **have** given me a lot of encourage-

S ~ V

ment. Checking the mailbox **is** the most exciting moment every day.

S ~ V

Making new friends **is** a good way to help me adapt myself to a new environment. I have

S ~ V ~ S ~ V

friends from different countries, which **include** England, Japan, Thailand, and Korea. Through

S ~ V ~ S ~ V

my friends I can learn about new cultures. All of my friends **are** the precious gifts in my life.

Summary Exercise c

Students work in pairs to identify and correct subject-verb agreement in each other's writing.

Summary Exercise d

Students check their own papers for subject-verb agreement.

Chapter 19: Agreement with Quantifiers

Exercise 1a

1. are
2. is
3. teach
4. possess
5. is
6. serve
7. bequeath
8. are
9. are
10. is

Exercise 1b

Gender Bias in America's Classrooms

Many of the recent studies on gender bias **confirm** that discrimination against female students still **occurs** frequently in American classrooms. Some of the elementary and secondary classroom teachers across the nation **believe** this is impossible. Nonetheless, every one of the studies **reveals** that many of our teachers **give** more attention to male students than to female students. In addition, it has been found that much of the curriculum **ignores** or **stereotypes** females. A lot of the gender bias in classrooms **undermines** girls' confidence and **dissuades** them from taking math and science courses. As a result, none of our female students **hopes** to escape the discrimination that subtly **discourages** them from participating in education as freely as their male counterparts. Studies have, in fact, revealed that most of the boys in America's elementary and secondary classrooms **speak** out eight times more often than the girls.

Exercise 1c

Traditional China

China is a traditional country where many of the ideas about boys and girls **are** based on age-old customs. According to tradition, many of the girls in the family **have** to do a lot of the housework, and most of them **are** not allowed to pursue a higher education. A lot of parents **feel** that their daughters won't rebel against parents' wishes if they are without education. A long time ago in Shanghai, many of the girls **had** bandaged feet so that they couldn't go outside. By contrast, the boys have better positions than girls. All of the boys **don't** do any housework, and most of them **are** encouraged to get a good education. Chinese parents still support the education of their sons even if one of the sons' ability **is** not very high. Parents always think the boys are more capable than the girls. Those different positions are unfair for girls.

Exercise 1d

Students practice using agreement with quantifiers in a paragraph.

Exercise 1e

Students edit each other's work for subject-verb agreement and use of quantifiers.

Chapter 20: Paired Conjunctions

Exercise 1a

1. Not only the president but also the vice president **has** given speeches about reinventing and improving government.

2. Neither the president nor the vice president **wants** to make false promises to the electorate.

3. Either Channel 4 or Channel 2 **televises** the campaign speeches and debates.

4. Not only important political advisors but also important members of both political parties **are** always present at these political events.

5. Not only newspaper reporters but also television reporters **are** eager to attend political debates.

6. Not only writers in national newspapers but also guests on television talk shows **analyze** and **discuss** the details of the political speeches and debates.

7. Both the news media and the print media **keep** the people informed about political issues and promises.

8. In many speeches both the president and the vice-president **have** promised to reform the health-care system.

9. Neither the younger voters nor the older voters **want** to continue paying high taxes without benefits.

Exercise 1b

1. Both the United States and Hong Kong have four seasons.
2. Not only Japanese cars but also Korean cars are economical.
3. Both Italian cooking and Spanish cooking are often spicy.
4. Neither the Chinese nor the Japanese drink coffee.
5. Both coffee and tea are available in American restaurants.

Exercise 1c

Students practice using paired conjunctions in writing about their countries. They should think about subject-verb agreement.

Exercise 1d

Students practice using paired conjunctions in writing about school life here and in their countries.

Chapter 21: Separated Subjects and Verbs

Exercise 1a

1. love
2. play
3. is played
4. is
5. is

Exercise 1b

Bicycle Safety

Many bicycle accidents involving children **occur** on quiet residential streets. However, these accidents, which cause thousands of visits to the emergency room annually, **are** preventable. Therefore, bicycle safety education for children **is** vital to the well-being of all young people. The causes of most bicycle accidents **are** riding into main roads without stopping and turning onto other roads without yielding. Furthermore, children, who are more vulnerable to injury than adults, **have** undeveloped peripheral vision, poor judgment of speed, and a distinct lack of a sense of danger. While it is a fact that an impact to the head can lead to serious injury, many parents do not insist that their children wear helmets. Parents who understand the facts about bicycles and safety **make** their children wear helmets. Helmets on children riding bicycles save lives!

Exercise 1c

Students work with their own writing and the writing of other students to create subject-verb agreement.

Chapter 22: *Other, Others,* and *Another* as Pronouns and Adjectives

Exercise 1a

1. The other
2. Others
3. The others

Exercise 1b

Students will have a variety of possible answers in this exercise, in which they practice using *others, the others,* and *the other* in sentences.

Exercise 1c

Students practice using the pronouns *others, the others,* and *the other* in paragraphs.

Exercise 2a

1. The other
2. Other
3. The other

Exercise 2b

Students practice using the adjectives *another, other,* and *the other* in sentences.

Exercise 2c

Students practice using the adjectives *another, other,* or *the other* in paragraphs.

Summary Exercise

Reasons I Miss the Spring in Japan

There are many reasons why I miss the springtime in Japan. When the spring flowers such as tulips and daffodils start to bloom in the northeast of the United States, I remember two wonderful aspects of spring in Japan. One is the small pink petals of the cherry blossoms, and <u>the other</u> (pronoun) is the sweet smell of the blooms. The cherry blossom is the national flower of Japan, and it seems to me that the Japanese love the cherry blossoms best among all flowers.

During the spring in Japan many people celebrate in many ways. One way is to pack a picnic lunch and go to the park. <u>Another</u> (adjective) way they enjoy celebrating is to sing to karaoke and dance. There are stands along the sidewalks which sell food and collectibles to the passersby. Some sell sweets and hot noodles. <u>Others</u> (pronoun) sell old-fashioned toys and spring plants.

Regardless of age or gender, everybody enjoys the short period of cherry trees in full bloom. At night the blossoms are lit up by lights placed between the trees. In the dim light some people find the world very romantic; <u>others</u> (pronoun) think it is mysterious. The ponds quietly reflect the cherry blossoms and the lamplight. Although I feel sad that the pink petals fall so soon, one senses the beauty of transience, which the Japanese feel is worth it. Sentimentality is the reason for the popularity of cherry blossoms in Japan.

Chapter 23: Demonstrative Adjectives

Exercise 1a

1. these
2. These
3. This, those
4. This
5. This

Exercise 1b

Students practice using the forms of *this, these, that,* and *those* in sentences.

Exercise 1c

Students check their papers in progress for demonstrative adjectives.

Chapter 24: Adjectives in a Series

Exercise 1a

1. We have seen <u>many wonderful ground-feeding</u> birds outside <u>our</u> house at <u>our bird</u> feeder.

2. There are usually <u>several big black</u> birds that come to <u>our bird</u> feeder during the <u>cold win-</u> ter months.

3. <u>The</u> kind of <u>bird</u> food and the type of <u>bird</u> feeder you choose will determine the <u>different</u> vari- eties of birds that will come to <u>the</u> feeder.

4. <u>Small</u> feeders will attract <u>small, delicate</u> birds; <u>large, heavy</u> birds will feed at <u>big</u> feeders.

5. All <u>the</u> birds enjoy <u>the</u> shelter of <u>our many beautiful tall oak shade</u> trees.

DETERMINER	QUALITY	SIZE	COLOR	MATERIAL	QUALIFYING NOUN
many	wonderful	big	black	oak	ground-feeding
our	cold	small			bird
several	different	large			winter
the	delicate	heavy			shade
	beautiful	tall			

Exercise 1b

Students practice writing sentences with adjectives in the correct order.

Exercise 1c

Students edit a partner's writing by using more adjectives.

Exercise 1d

Students use a paper in progress to identify nouns and add appropriate adjectives.

Chapter 25: Fragments

Exercise 1

1. fragment; are interested
2. fragment; is changing
3. fragment; Technology began . . .
4. fragment; By improving the field of communication, we have improved our lives.
5. fragment; is now possible
6. fragment; Communication has improved . . .
7. complete
8. complete
9. fragment; is improving
10. fragment; are working

Exercise 2

1. In retailing, "impulse" purchases are small, inexpensive items that are found near the cash registers and checkout lanes of stores.

2. According to a consumer analyst, eating dinner out is an impulse purchase for most Americans.

3. For over 50 percent of Americans, the decision to eat out is made on the spur of the moment.

4. Although they would prefer to eat home cooking, many people end up eating out because it saves time.

5. Even if restaurants were easily affordable, a large number of people would prefer eating at home.

6. While many people eat out because it is easier, others eat out to socialize with friends.

7. Young adults eat in fast-food restaurants more often than older Americans, despite the fact that older, more affluent Americans eat in expensive restaurants most often.

8. Because Americans give in to their food impulses, most restaurant meals are bought on impulse.

Exercise 3a

1. Because friendships have been shown to be crucial to our health and well-being, people are encouraged to seek the support and affection of friends to ease the daily stress of our lives.

   Friendships have been shown to be crucial to our health and well-being. People are encouraged to seek the support and affection of friends to ease the daily stress of our lives.

2. In fact, people who have friends are less likely to suffer from disease, knowing they can turn to others for advice and affection.

   In fact, people who have friends are less likely to suffer from disease. They know they can turn to others for advice and affection.

3. Furthermore, those who are afflicted with disease are quicker to recover when they have friendship and support.

   Furthermore, those who are afflicted with disease are quicker to recover, having friendship and support.

4. For example, in a study of heart patients, those patients who lacked a spouse or confidant recovered more slowly than those who had a strong support group.

   For example, a study of heart patients showed that those patients who lacked a spouse or confidant recovered more slowly than those who had a strong support group.

5. Support groups may be as powerful as medicine. One of the most important influences on healing is being among loving friends.

   Support groups may be as powerful as medicine, among the most important influences on healing the need to be among loving friends.

6. Yet in the busy and very mobile lives of most Americans, making and maintaining friend-ships can sometimes be difficult.

   Making and maintaining friendships can sometimes be difficult in the busy and very mobile lives of most Americans.

7. Friendships are still a vital part of living a happy and healthy life, although it can be a chal-lenge to keep long-distance relationships.

   Friendships are still a vital part of living a happy and healthy life; it can be a challenge to keep long-distance relationships.

Exercise 3b

Students search for fragments in newspapers, magazines, or textbooks, and they think of strategies to correct the fragments.

Exercise 3c

Students practice writing, then editing for fragments.

Chapter 26: Comma Splices and Fused Sentences

Exercise 1

1. _____fs_____ Surveys reveal that 15 to 20 percent of all drivers have fallen asleep while driving at least once in their lives**//**most of the drivers wake up before having an accident.

2. _____cs_____ Driver fatigue is one of the most common factors in car crashes**,** one-third of fatal truck accidents are caused by drivers falling asleep at the wheel.

3. _____fs_____ The hectic life-style of Americans is part of the problem**//**more and more people are rushing between home, work, and school.

4. _____fs_____ Holding two jobs or working at night can make people very susceptible to drowsi-ness**//**these people may easily fall asleep at the wheel.

5. _____cs_____ Remaining alert is vital to driver safety**,** driving while drowsy is as dangerous as driving while drinking.

6. _____fs_____ Highway authorities have started to install "rumble strips" on the edges of high-ways**//**the strips make a sound and wake up a driver who may have fallen asleep.

7. _____fs_____ People need to respect the body's signals to stop driving**//**precautions such as resting, listening to the radio, or stopping for a short walk should be taken.

8. _____fs_____ Drivers who are very tired need to stop driving for a short roadside nap**//**they can also drink coffee or chew gum.

9. _____fs_____ Everyone has been aware that drinking and driving is dangerous**//**it is time that people understood the dangers of driving while fatigued.

10. _____fs_____ A good driver needs to be alert and to feel rested**//**this should be considered when-ever someone gets behind the wheel.

Exercise 2a

1. Halloween was originally a Celtic festival for the dead **, and** it was celebrated on the last day of the Celtic year, October 31.

   Halloween was originally a Celtic festival for the dead **;** it was celebrated on the last day of the Celtic year, October 31.

2. In Europe, huge bonfires were built to ward off evil spirits **.** It was believed that witches and goblins were everywhere.

   In Europe, huge bonfires were built to ward off evil spirits **, and** it was believed that witches and goblins were everywhere.

3. Today in America, the holiday is a festival of costumes and pumpkin carving **;** in many towns across the United States people leave jack-o'-lanterns outside their doors to keep away ghosts and spirits.

   Today in America, the holiday is a festival of costumes and pumpkin carving; **in fact,** in many towns across the United States people leave jack-o'-lanterns outside their doors to keep away ghosts and spirits.

4. In fact, this is done only for fun **, so** many people wait for children dressed up in costumes to come to their doors "trick-or-treating."

   In fact, this is done only for fun **;** many people wait for children dressed up in costumes to come to their doors "trick-or-treating."

5. Children wear scary costumes and carry bags for treats **;** **in addition,** they play tricks on people who don't give them candies.

   Children wear scary costumes and carry bags for treats **, so** they play tricks on people who don't give them candies.

6. They enjoy walking in the dark trick-or-treating **.** Children visit haunted houses for fun, too.

   They enjoy walking in the dark trick-or-treating **;** children visit haunted houses for fun, too.

7. Children enjoy the excitement of pretend ghosts and goblins **, so** this holiday makes these activities fun for all!

   Because children enjoy the excitement of pretend ghosts and goblins **,** this holiday makes these activities fun for all!

Exercise 2b

Students can use varying methods to revise comma splices and fused sentences and improve the paragraph.

Exercise 2c

Students practice writing in a freewriting exercise.

Exercise 2d

Students edit each other's writing for comma splices and fused sentences.

Chapter 27: Parallelism

Exercise 1a

1. I came to the United States, I saw many new and unusual sights, and I conquered the new life-style. clauses

2. I hoped to meet many people and to learn many things in the United States. phrases

3. At first the climate and the cuisine seemed very different. words

4. Then, I had to adjust to the new language, accommodate to the new culture, and integrate the new customs. phrases

5. Soon I realized that living in a new country and embracing a new culture were essential to learning a new language. phrases

6. I decided that I should get to know people who were familiar with the new culture and who were fluent in the new language. phrases

7. How to meet people and where to meet people were my two problems. phrases

8. I consciously went to the library, the cafeteria, and the gym as often as possible. words

9. In no time I had met a lot of interesting people, and I had begun to feel at home in my new country. clauses

10. Live and learn—I had found that life was exciting, challenging, and worthwhile. words

Exercise 1b

1. It is important to note that life changed dramatically for early humans when they learned to use fire and caves.

2. It is believed that the cold prompted them to take embers from a natural fire and bring it to a cave.

3. They used fire to chase the animals in a hunt, to protect themselves when they rested, and to harden their spears.

4. But the wonder of fire was more than warmth, more than protection, and more than practical help in making weapons.

5. The wonder of fire was that it lengthened the daylight hours, it allowed people to work at night, and it gave people an opportunity to sit by the fire and talk.

6. The fire also gave early humans a sense of home where there was comfort, security, and family.

7. The keeper of the fire was probably a member of the clan who was older and wiser.

8. The old ones had survived difficulties, avoided accidents, and used their intelligence to reach old age.

9. The cave gave the early people a place to make tools, to store food, and to cure animal hides.

10. Later on, these cave dwellers began painting on the walls and using their fires for ceremonies.

Exercise 1c

Students write sentences using words, phrases, and clauses in parallel form.

Exercise 2

1. The Caribbean Basin is isolated from other world waters **and** has different wildlife.

2. This body of water is bordered by Central and South America **and** by the Atlantic Ocean.

3. The barrier of land prevents migration of tropical marine species**,** **and** the barrier of cold water prevents migration of tropical marine species.

4. Because of the isolation of the waters **and** the evolution of separate wildlife, the marine species of the Caribbean Basin are unique.

5. The spectacular flora and fauna are appreciated by professional **and** amateur divers.

6. Environmentalists hope to preserve the area's natural beauty**,** **for** the Caribbean Basin has become increasingly popular.

7. Awareness of the fragile quality of marine life **and** realization of the need to preserve this wildlife should help prevent destruction of the area.

8. Divers who enjoy **and** appreciate the beautiful Caribbean Basin must respect this delicate balance.

Exercise 3

Students will have a variety of possible answers using correlative conjunctions to form parallel sentence elements.

Summary Exercise a

1. I miss my beautiful, powerful, **and** successful country, China.

2. Japan has maintained not only high technology **but also** a beautiful culture and strong spirit.

3. The landscape makes you half tipsy, the people make you feel warm, **and** the word *China* leads you into a Xanadu.

4. I love Taiwan because it is the place where I was born **and** the place where I live.

5. Russia, my ardently loved motherland, has not only a long history **but also** many wonders with fascinating scenery.

6. Mexico's economy is growing, its technology is advancing, **and** its education is improving.

7. There are a lot of beautiful places, interesting stories, **and** delicious foods in Thailand.

8. The birds are singing, the flowers are giving off fragrant smells, **and** the trees are growing— all are the nature of my country, Korea.

9. My country, Pakistan, has beautiful cities, exciting hillsides, **and** soothing beaches.

10. Japan has four seasons, which are green spring, blue summer, yellow fall, **and** white winter.

11. My country is very famous for great sight-seeing in Dae-Gu, the beautiful ocean in Pu-San, **and** delicious food in Cheon-An.

12. Ukraine is beautiful in its traditions, rich in its natural resources, **and** friendly in its people.

13. The Kunlun mountain range is her body; the Great Wall is her backbone; the Yellow River is her blood; the capital, Beijing, is her heart. She is just my own country—China.

14. Coming to my country, Vietnam, tourists can enjoy beautiful weather, taste different tropical fruits, **and** visit many clean white beaches all year round.

Summary Exercise 1b

Students write sentences about their countries, using the ideas of parallel structure in this chapter.

Summary Exercise c

Students share their sentences from Summary Exercise b, looking for parallel elements.

Summary Exercise d

Students analyze the thesis statement in a paper in progress, then revise it to use parallel structure.

Chapter 28: Coordination and Subordination

Exercise 1a

1. Nevada is the only western state where gambling is legal, **and** many people come to gamble and to see the celebrities who perform in this state.

   Nevada is the only western state where gambling is legal; **in addition,** many people come to gamble and to see the celebrities who perform in this state.

   Nevada is the only western state where gambling is legal; many people come to gamble and to see the celebrities who perform in this state.

2. Utah has many wonderful national parks, canyons, and deserts, **and** Utah has the famous Salt Lake, which is four times as salty as any ocean.

   Utah has many wonderful national parks, canyons, and deserts; **furthermore,** Utah has the famous Salt Lake, which is four times as salty as any ocean.

   Utah has many wonderful national parks, canyons, and deserts; Utah has the famous Salt Lake, which is four times as salty as any ocean.

3. Washington's largest city, Seattle, is one of America's most popular cities, **so** it is a growing state.

   Washington's largest city, Seattle, is one of America's most popular cities; **therefore,** it is a growing state.

   Washington's largest city, Seattle, is one of America's most popular cities; it is a growing state.

4. Tennessee is famous for the birth of America's music, **and** Elvis Presley, the famous king of rock and roll, lived in Tennessee.

   Tennessee is famous for the birth of America's music; **moreover,** Elvis Presley, the famous king of rock and roll, lived in Tennessee.

   Tennessee is famous for the birth of America's music; Elvis Presley, the famous king of rock and roll, lived in Tennessee.

5. New Orleans, located in Louisiana, is one of America's busiest ports, **and** jazz was first played in this state.

   New Orleans, located in Louisiana, is one of America's busiest ports; **in addition,** jazz was first played in this state.

   New Orleans, located in Louisiana, is one of America's busiest ports; jazz was first played in this state.

Exercise 1b

Students can use any of the three methods of forming compound sentences from Exercise 1a. There will be a variety of possible answers.

Exercise 2a

1. Pennsylvania is famous for chocolate **because** the world's largest chocolate and cocoa factory is in Hershey, Pennsylvania.

2. North Carolina is famous for flying **since** the first successful air flight in the world took place in this state.

3. The world's first atomic bomb was set off in New Mexico in 1945 **after** this bomb was built in that state.

4. **Although** the world's first professional baseball game was played in Hoboken, New Jersey, few people realize this event happened in New Jersey.

5. **Even though** Kentucky is most often thought of as Abraham Lincoln's birthplace, Kentucky has the world's largest Braille publishing house.

Exercise 2b

Students use different subordinators to form complex sentences as in Exercise 2a. There will be a variety of possible answers.

Exercise 3

1. (While) millions of tourists come to California each year, they visit Hollywood, Disneyland, and Death Valley, (and) they visit the giant sequoia trees, which are the largest living things in the world.

2. Texas is the second-largest state in the United States, (and) (since) many famous cowboys lived and died in Texas, this state is famous for cowboys and rodeos.

3. (Although) Ohio was the birthplace of eight U.S. presidents, other famous people came from Ohio, (and) Thomas A. Edison, the Wright brothers, and John D. Rockefeller, Sr., were all born in this state.

4. Michigan is known for manufacturing more trucks and cars than any other state, (and) (because) it also has eleven thousand lakes, it has the longest suspension bridge, which connects two parts of the state.

5. New York State has the biggest city in the country, (but) (since) New York has huge national parklands as well, outdoor sports enthusiasts visit these parklands every year in all seasons.

Summary Exercise a

Students practice using coordination and subordination to combine sentences. There will be a variety of possible answers.

Summary Exercise b

Students analyze a paper in progress and revise for coordination and subordination.

Chapter 29: Strategies for Spelling

Exercise 1a

1. mottoes
2. estuaries
3. chemistries
4. turkeys
5. lives
6. phenomena
7. mothers-in-law
8. footballs
9. women
10. studios

Exercise 1b

1. impossible
2. unhelpful
3. unbelievable
4. unhappy
5. imperceptible
6. unreliable
7. intolerable
8. improper
9. unlucky
10. inappropriate

Exercise 1c

1. understandable
2. believable
3. peaceful
4. usable, useful
5. helpful
6. definable
7. plentiful
8. hopeful
9. readable
10. irrepressible

Exercise 1d

1. stayed, staying
2. weeded, weeding
3. handed, handing
4. dried, drying
5. typed, typing
6. referred, referring
7. loved, loving
8. abided, abiding
9. studied, studying
10. learned, learning

Exercise 2

1. bored
2. role
3. thought
4. weather
5. environment
6. lose, studying
7. past, a lot, its
8. accept
9. quite, afford
10. facility

Exercise 3a

Students think of a variety of ways to remember the spellings of some troublesome words.

Exercise 3b

Students keep a notebook of their most often misspelled words. They might share this information with each other.

Exercise 3c

Students check spelling in their own papers.

Chapter 30: Editing Student Writing for Punctuation, Spelling, and Capitalization

Exercise 1a

My Future Wife Must Have Three Characteristics

Marriage is one of the most important decisions we make in our lives. I think the reason is that we are not meant to live alone. When I get **married,** my wife must have three characteristics: a compromising attitude, an intelligent mind, and a smile.

A compromising attitude will give people a good relationship. Marriage is a relationship that may last for thirty years or more. Although I can't promise that I won't fight at all with my wife over the years, I will certainly try to make compromises. Sometimes couples can't get along, and if we **treat** each other with a kind attitude, we will work it out peacefully.

We are living in a society that is very complex, and decisions have to be made all the time. We can't always know the right answer to our problems, but if my wife is intelligent, she can be a great help to me. We can share our knowledge of the world and live an intelligent life together.

I think the most beautiful thing is a smile. Whenever I glance at someone's smile, I feel comfortable, as if I have been blessed. A smile that comes from the heart brings a feeling of kindness. I would love to see the smile of my wife whenever I come home or wherever I am. I would forget all sorts of stress from life, work, and so on.

A compromising spirit, an intelligent attitude, and a beautiful smile are the **qualities** I want in my future spouse. Do you have any idea what else I need?

Exercise 1b

Traditional Festivity

Chinese New Year is the most important and meaningful festivity for all Chinese **people.** All Chinese people believe that the coming of the new year means **changing** the old things for the new, and also **changing** the bad things for the good. Therefore, all people will treasure that day's coming, and they will celebrate it.

New **Y**ear is a busy time for all **C**hinese people, especially women, who have to clean the house and prepare the food for the new year. Everybody hopes to live in **happier** conditions in the new year. When the women clean the dirt out of the house, they hope to clean out the bad luck as well.

New **Y**ear is a time for people to have a delicious meal and be together with all the family. The New **Y**ear dinner, which is prepared and eaten on New Year's **E**ve, is one very important part of the **celebration** because it is the last meal of the old year. According to Chinese tradition, the whole family must gather together and enjoy the pleasure of a happy home circle. After the family **finishes** the dinner, everybody gets dressed up in new clothing.

Chinese New Year is also very much a holiday for **children.** Because they get to eat delicious food and dress up in new clothing, children choose this holiday as their favorite holiday. In addition, parents and **married** relatives give children "lucky money," which is put in little red pouches. Finally, children are given more freedom during the New Year holiday, and their parents **rarely** punish them at this time.

Exercise 1c

Freedom for Catalonia

Catalonia is a very small country. It is older than the United States, and it has been invaded many times. The last time was in 1936, when my grandfathers were between twenty and thirty years old and my father was only six months old. The army of Spain had invaded Catalonia, and there was a war for two years. During these two years, a lot of Catalan people were executed, the Catalon language was **forbidden,** and the King of Spain was exiled. The president of Catalonia **escaped** to France, and General Francisco Franco established a dictatorship.

One of my grandfathers was in prison for a very long time, but they didn't **execute** him because he knew **a lot** of people. Both of my grandfathers are obsessed about the war, and they often explain the **history** of that time. General Franco died when I was seven years old, and now there is a democracy in Spain. Catalonia is not a free country yet, but we have our own government and **president.**

Exercise 1d

The U.S.A.

I would like to write a paragraph about a country where I live, work, and study. In America I see a country of opportunity and education. America is a country of freedom; **in fact,** it is a country where everything is **possible.** My major is **biology,** and in the future, I would like to study **medicine.** In my view, the United States is one of the best **countries** in which to study medicine, and this is connected to the excellent medical **technology** in this country. I was surprised when I saw all the machines people were **using.** Medicine in America is strong and powerful. We live in a country that has a great future.

Index